Kira Salak was born in Illinois in 1971. She has a Ph.D. in English and Creative Writing from the University of Missouri at Columbia, and frequently travels to the world's furthest-flung places on assignment for *National Geographic*. She also writes for *National Geographic Adventure*, *New York Times Magazine* and a host of literary travel journals. Her first book, *Four Corners: A Journey to the Heart of Papua New Guinea*, was chosen by the *New York Times Book Review* as a Notable Travel Book of the Year. In 2004 she was awarded the PEN Literary Award in Journalism and the Lowell Thomas Gold Award for Travel Journalism. Her work has appeared in *Best New American Voices* and *Best American Travel Writing 2002, 2003* and *2004*. Kira Salak lives in Montana.

www.booksattransworld.co.uk

*Also by Kira Salak*

FOUR CORNERS: A Journey to the Heart
of Papua New Guinea

*and published by Bantam Books*

# THE CRUELLEST JOURNEY

600 miles in a canoe to the legendary
city of Timbuktu

# Kira Salak

**BANTAM BOOKS**

LONDON • TORONTO • SYDNEY • AUCKLAND • JOHANNESBURG

**THE CRUELLEST JOURNEY**
**A BANTAM BOOK : 0 553 81629 2**

Originally published in Great Britain by Bantam Press,
a division of Transworld Publishers

PRINTING HISTORY
Bantam Press edition published 2005
Bantam edition published 2006

1 3 5 7 9 10 8 6 4 2

Set in 12/15pt Granjon by
Falcon Oast Graphic Art Ltd.

Bantam Books are published by Transworld Publishers,
61–63 Uxbridge Road, London W5 5SA,
a division of The Random House Group Ltd,
in Australia by Random House Australia (Pty) Ltd,
20 Alfred Street, Milsons Point, Sydney, NSW 2061, Australia,
in New Zealand by Random House New Zealand Ltd,
18 Poland Road, Glenfield, Auckland 10, New Zealand
and in South Africa by Random House (Pty) Ltd,
Isle of Houghton, Corner Boundary Road & Carse O'Gowrie,
Houghton 2198, South Africa.

Printed and bound in Great Britain by
Cox & Wyman Ltd, Reading, Berkshire.

Papers used by Transworld Publishers are natural, recyclable
products made from wood grown in sustainable forests. The
manufacturing processes conform to the environmental
regulations of the country of origin.

*For my mother and her own journey, with love*

And I tell you, if you have the desire for knowledge and the power to give it physical expression, go out and explore . . . Some will tell you that you are mad, and nearly all will say, 'What is the use?' For we are a nation of shopkeepers, and no shopkeeper will look at research which does not promise him a financial return within a year. And so you will sledge nearly alone, but those with whom you sledge will not be shopkeepers: that is worth a great deal. If you march your Winter Journeys you will have your reward, so long as all you want is a penguin's egg.

— Apsley Cherry-Garrard, from
*The Worst Journey in the World*

*The winds roared, and the rains fell.*
*The poor white man, faint and weary, came*
    *and sat under our tree.*
*He has no mother to bring him milk; no wife*
    *to grind his corn.*
*Let us pity the white man; no mother has he.*

— Native ballad written about
Mungo Park, Ségou Korro, 1796

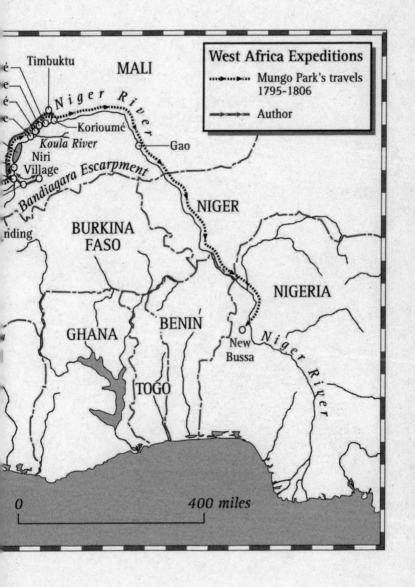

Timbuktu

MALI

_Niger River_

Korioumé

_Koula River_

Niri
Village

_Bandiagara Escarpment_

Gao

nding

BURKINA
FASO

NIGER

GHANA

BENIN

NIGERIA

TOGO

New
Bussa

_Niger River_

**West Africa Expeditions**

··►··►··►·· Mungo Park's travels
1795–1806

─►─►─►─ Author

_0_                  _400 miles_

# PROLOGUE

*Wide Afric, doth thy sun*
*Lighten, thy hills unfold a city as fair*
*As those which starred the night o' the elder world?*
*Or is the rumour of thy Timbuctoo*
*A dream as frail as those of ancient time?*
—Tennyson, 'Timbuctoo'

I CAN'T IMAGINE TIMBUKTU HERE. I STAY IN ANOTHER OF the world's cheap hotel rooms, this time in Mali, West Africa, in the capital city of Bamako. Cockroaches crouch behind the cracked porcelain toilet bowl; beetles climb the walls; mosquitoes hover over me, half dazed. Unsavoury couples check into rooms next door, checking out a couple of hours later. But I'm fortunate because my room includes a shower, however basic, with a weary trickle of water. The electricity goes out at 9 a.m. sharp, turning off a rickety overhead fan, allowing the heat to filter through a pitted screen over the window and settle on my skin like a balm. I lie on a thin green cotton bedspread, wondering when it was last washed, trying to guess the source of the various stains on it. The frenetic sound of Bamako traffic invades through the wooden shutters that I always keep closed over the window. I hear a crashing sound from cars on the street – the usual, familiar crashing sound that I only seem to hear from such rooms – followed by yells in incensed Bambarra. Then, once again, the growls of passing motorbikes and the return of the dull, featureless milling of crowds.

I roll on to my side, listening, studying, trying to memorize the poverty. The bloody smears of dead mosquitoes on the whitewashed wall before me. A floor that, if stepped on, leaves dust and strangers' hairs and fallen stucco from the ceiling clinging to the soles of my feet. A TV roaring from the room of the guy down the hall, whose job it is to clean these rooms, though of course he only makes the beds. The toilet smelling strongly of piss. The bed reeking of mildew and pungent sweat. The sink drip-dripping water with the certainty of a clock's second hand.

Very little changes about these rooms except the languages I hear through the window, or the colour of the bedspreads, or the wattage of the single overhead light bulb. These are rooms that wake me in the middle of the night. Rooms that hold their darkness in gravid pause. Rooms that require sleeping pills because I so badly want the day back. They tell me when it's time to leave. They start all my journeys.

# CHAPTER ONE

IN THE BEGINNING, MY JOURNEYS FEEL AT BEST ludicrous, at worst insane. This one is no exception. The idea is to paddle nearly six hundred miles on the Niger River in a kayak, alone, from the Malian town of Old Ségou to Timbuktu. And now, at the very hour when I have decided to leave, a thunderstorm bursts open the skies, sending down apocalyptic rain, washing away the very ground beneath my feet. It is the rainy season in Mali, for which there can be no comparison in the world. Lightning pierces trees, slices across houses. Thunder racks the skies and pounds the earth like mortar fire, and every living thing huddles in tenuous shelter, expecting the world to end. Which it doesn't. At least not this time. So that we all give a collective sigh to the salvation from the passing storm as it rumbles its way east, and I survey the river I'm to leave on this morning. Rain or no rain, today is the day for the journey to begin. And no-one, not even the oldest in the village, can say for certain whether I'll get to the end.

'Let's do it,' I say, leaving the shelter of an adobe hut. My guide from town, Modibo, points to the north, to further storms. He says he will pray for me. It's the best he can do. To his knowledge, no man has ever completed such a trip, though a few have tried. And certainly no woman has done such a thing. This morning he took me aside and told me he thinks I'm crazy, which I understood as concern and thanked him. He told me that the people of Old Ségou think I'm crazy too, and that only uncanny good luck will keep me safe.

Still, when a person tells me I can't do something, I'll want to do it all the more. It may be a failing of mine. I carry my inflatable kayak through the narrow passageways of Old Ségou, past the small adobe huts melting in the rains, past the huddling goats and smoke of cooking fires, people peering out at me from the dark entranceways. It is a labyrinth of ancient homes, built and rebuilt after each storm, plastered with the very earth people walk upon. Old Ségou must look much the same as it did in Scottish explorer Mungo Park's time when, exactly 206 years ago to the day, he left on the first of his two river journeys down the Niger to Timbuktu, the first such attempt by a Westerner. It is no coincidence that I've planned to leave on the same day and from the same spot. Park is my benefactor of sorts, my guarantee. If he could travel down the Niger, then so can I. And it is all the guarantee I have for this trip – that an obsessed nineteenth-century adventurer did what I would like to do. Of course Park also died on this river, but so far I've managed to overlook that.

I gaze at the Niger through the adobe passageways, staring at waters that began in the mountainous rain forests of Guinea and travelled all this way to central Mali – waters that will journey north-east with me to Timbuktu before cutting a great circular swath through the Sahara and retreating south, through Niger, on to Nigeria, passing circuitously through mangrove swamps and jungle, resting at last in the Atlantic in the Bight of Benin. But the Niger is more than a river; it is a kind of faith. Bent and plied by Saharan sands, it perseveres more than 2,600 miles from beginning to end through one of the hottest, most desolate regions of the world. And when the rains come each year, it finds new strength of purpose, surging through the sun-baked lands, giving people the boons of crops and livestock and fish, taking nothing, asking nothing. It humbles all who see it.

If I were to try to explain why I'm here, why I chose Mali and the Niger for this journey – now that is a different matter. I can already feel the resistance in my gut, the familiar clutch of fear. I used to avoid stripping myself down in search of motivation, scared of what I might uncover, scared of anything that might suggest a taint of the pathological. And would it be enough to say that I admire Park's own trip on the river and want to try a similar challenge? That answer carries a whiff of the disingenuous; it sounds too easy to me. Human motivation, itself, is a complicated thing. Would it were simple enough to say,

'Here is the Niger, and I want to paddle it.' But I'm not that kind of traveller, and this isn't that kind of trip. If a journey doesn't have something to teach you about yourself, then what kind of journey is it? There is one thing I'm already certain of: though we may think we choose our journeys, they choose us.

Hobbled donkeys cower under a new onslaught of rain, ears back, necks craned. Little naked children dare each other to touch me, and I make it easy for them, stopping and holding out my arm. They stroke my white skin as if it were velvet, using only the pads of their fingers, then stare at their hands to check for wet paint.

Thunder again. More rain falls. I stop on the shore, near a centuries-old kapok tree under which I imagine Park once took shade. I open my bag, spread out my little red kayak, and start to pump it up. I'm doing this trip under the sponsorship of *National Geographic Adventure*, which hopes to run a magazine story about it. This means that they need photos, lots of photos, and so a French photographer named Rémi Bénali feverishly snaps pictures of me. I don't know what I hate more – river storms or photo shoots. I value the privacy and integrity of my trips, don't want my journey turning into a circus. The magazine presented the best compromise it could: Rémi, renting a motor-driven pirogue, was given instructions to find me on the river every few days to do his job.

My kayak is nearly inflated. A couple of women nearby, with colourful cloth wraps called *pagnes* tied tightly about their breasts, gaze at me cryptically, as if to ask: *Who are you and what do you think you're doing?* The Niger churns and slaps the shore, in a surly mood. I don't pretend to know what I'm doing. Just one thing at a time now, kayak inflated, kayak loaded with my gear. Paddles fitted together and ready. Modibo is standing on the shore, watching me.

'I'll pray for you,' he reminds me.

I balance my gear, adjust the straps, get in. And finally, irrevocably, I paddle away.

When Mungo Park left on his second trip, he never admitted that he was scared. It is what fascinates me about his writing – his insistence on maintaining an illusion that all was well, even as he began a journey that he knew from previous experience could only beget tragedy. Hostile peoples, unknown rapids, malarial fevers. Hippos and crocodiles. The giant Lake Debo to cross, like being set adrift on an inland sea, no sight of land, no way of knowing where the river starts again. Forty of his forty-four men dead from sickness, Park himself afflicted with dysentery when he left on this trip. And it can boggle the mind, what drives some people to risk their lives for the mute promises of success. Already I fear the irrationality of my journey, the relentless stubbornness that drives me on.

The storm erupts into a new overture. Torrential rains. Waves higher than my kayak, trying to capsize me. But my boat is self-bailing and I stay afloat. The wind drives the current in reverse, tearing and ripping at the shores, sending spray into my face. I paddle madly, crashing and driving forward. I travel inch by inch, or so it seems, arm muscles smarting and rebelling against the effort. I crawl past New Ségou, fighting the Niger for more distance. Large river steamers rest in jumbled rows before cement docks, the town itself looking dark and deserted in the downpour. No-one is out in a boat. The people know something I don't: that the river dictates all travel.

A popping feeling now and a screech of pain. My right arm lurches from a ripped muscle. But this is no time and place for such an injury, and I won't tolerate it, stuck as I am in a storm. I try to get used to the pulses of pain as I fight the river. There is only one direction to go: forward. Stopping has become anathema.

I wonder what we look for when we embark on these kinds of trips. There is the pat answer that you tell the people you don't know: that you're interested in seeing a place, learning about its people. But then the trip begins and the hardship comes, and hardship is more honest: it tells us that we don't have enough patience yet, nor humility, nor gratitude. And we thought that we had. Hardship brings us closer to truth, and thus is more difficult to bear, but from it alone comes compassion. And so I've told the world that it can do what it wants with me during this trip if only, by the end, I have learned something more. A bargain, then. The journey, my teacher.

And where is the river of just this morning, with its whitecaps that would have liked to drown me, with its current flowing backwards against the wind? Gone to this: a river of smoothest glass, a placidity unbroken by wave or eddy, with islands of lush greenery awaiting me like distant Xanadus. The Niger is like a mercurial god, meting out punishment and benediction on a whim. And perhaps the god of the river sleeps now, returning matters to the mortals who ply its waters? The Bozo and Somono fishermen in their pointy canoes. The long passenger pirogues, overloaded with people and merchandise, rumbling past, leaving diesel fumes in their wake. And now, inexplicably, the white woman in a little red boat, paddling through waters that flawlessly mirror the cumulus clouds above. We all belong here, in our way. It is as if I've entered a very lucid dream, continually surprised to find myself here on this river – I've become a hapless actor in a mysterious play, not yet knowing what my part is, left to gape at the wonder of what I have set in motion. Somehow: I'm in a kayak, on the Niger River, paddling very slowly but very surely to Timbuktu.

I pass tiny villages of adobe huts on the shores, some large and full of busy work: women washing clothes and dishes in the river, children chasing after goats, men repairing fishing nets. In other villages, some smaller and less permanent-looking, with huts made from mud and thatch, men lounge beneath trees and swat flies and talk. The women pound millet with wooden pestles the size of a small child. I get used to the certainty of their up-and-down movements, the *thump* of the pestle in the stone mortar, again and again, like a drumbeat. It is the music of rural Mali, as are the fervent calls of the children when I pass, and the great bellowing of donkeys that could surely be heard on the other side of the world. Each village has its own mud mosque sending squat minarets to the heavens. There is nothing glamorous about the architecture – no sharp angles or filigree or carvings – but it is this very unprepossessing quality that makes them special. Like mud castles of childhood fancy, they seem built from some latent creative energy, spiky sticks topping the minarets, ostrich eggs beacon-like on the highest points, with small portholes carved from the mud sides and staring out enigmatically at the traveller. The impulse is to stop and try to peek inside, to get a look at the dark interior, the primordial secrets within.

But I only pass by. The mosques in these parts probably wouldn't be open to me. Before my trip began, I asked to see one in a riverside village, and the imam solemnly shook his head. A reason was translated to me: I'm an 'infidel', a sinner. I would not even be allowed to climb the outside stairs. He also called me a Christian, and though he was incorrect (I practise Buddhism), I felt a tweaking in my stomach that was part anger, part sorrow: I had been summed up and dismissed in a matter of seconds. But surely it's human nature to overlook similarities for differences, people fortifying imaginary walls between themselves more insurmountable than any made from stone.

The late-afternoon sun settles complacently over the hills to the west. Paddling becomes a sort of meditation now, a gentle trespassing over a river that slumbers. The Niger gives me its beauty almost in apology for the violence of the earlier storms, treating me to smooth silver waters that ripple in the sunlight. The current – if there is one – barely moves. Park described the same grandeur during his second journey, in an uncharacteristically sentimental passage that provided a welcome respite from accounts of dying soldiers and baggage stolen by natives: 'We travelled very pleasantly all day; in fact nothing can be more beautiful than the views of this immense river; sometimes as smooth as a mirror, at other times ruffled with a gentle breeze, but at all times sweeping us along at the rate of six or seven miles per hour.'

I barely travel at one mile an hour, the river preferring – as I do – to loiter in the sun. I lean down in my seat and hang my feet over the sides of the kayak. I eat turkey jerky and wrap up my injured arm, part of which has swollen to the size of a grapefruit. I'm not worried about the injury any more. I'm not worried about anything. I know this feeling won't last, but for now I wrap myself in it, feeling the rare peace. To reach a place of not worrying is a greater freedom than anything I could hope to find on one of these trips. It is my true Undiscovered Country.

The Somono fishermen, casting out their nets, puzzle over me as I float by.

'Ça va, madame?' they yell.

Each fisherman carries a young son perched in the back of his pointed canoe to do the paddling. The boys stare at me, transfixed; they have never seen such a thing. A white woman. Alone. In a red, inflatable boat. Using a two-sided paddle.

I'm an even greater novelty because Malian women don't paddle, not ever. It is a man's job. So there is no good explanation for me, and the people want to understand. They want to see if I'm strong enough for it, or if I even know how to use a paddle. They want to determine how sturdy my boat is. They gather on the shore in front of their villages to watch me pass, the kids screaming and jumping in excitement, the women with hands to foreheads to shield the sun as they stare, men yelling out questions in Bambarra which by now I know to mean: 'Where did you come from? Are you alone? Where's your husband?' And of course they will always ask: 'Where are you going?'

'Timbuktu!' I yell out to the last question. Which sounds preposterous to them, because everyone knows that Timbuktu is weeks away, and requires paddling across Lake Debo somehow, and through rapids and storms. And I am a woman, after all, which must make everything worse.

'*Tombouctou?!*' they always repeat, just to be sure.

'*Awo*,' I say in the Bambarra I've learned. 'Yes.'

Head-shakes. Shared grins. We wave goodbye, and the whole ritual begins again at the next village. And at the next, and the next after that, kids running beside me along the shore, singing out their frantic choruses of '*Ça va! Ça va!*' I might be the Pope, or someone close. But in between is the peace and silence of the wide river, the sun on me, a breeze licking my toes when I lie back to rest, the current as negligible as a faint breath.

I think often about Mungo Park's journeys to this

country, which were anything but easy for him. But he was a tough young Scot, and had an impressive fortitude to endure hardship. Park was only twenty-three years old when he left on his first journey to West Africa in search of the Niger River and Timbuktu. He was not without striking, fascinating contradictions in character. He was by any standards a devoutly spiritual man, convinced that the vagaries of life have their place in God's scheme of things. He would write:

> The melancholy, who complain of the shortness of human life, and the voluptuous, who think the present only their own, strive to fill up every moment with sensual enjoyment; but the man whose soul has been enlightened by his Creator, and enabled, though dimly, to discern the wonders of salvation, will look upon the joys and afflictions of this life as equally the tokens of Divine love. He will walk through the world as one travelling to a better country, looking forward with wonder to the author and finisher of his faith.

But he was also a pragmatist who could be lured by the trappings of future fame, confiding in his brother that he would 'acquire a name greater than any ever did'. Was this merely explorer's hubris? Or was it also the source of Park's extraordinary ability to endure difficulty and danger?

During any kind of journey, when virtually nothing is within one's control, when nothing can be sufficiently anticipated or prepared for, a great deal of hubris is necessary. I must tell myself now, for example, that I can get to Timbuktu. I must say it as if it were already so, assuring myself that I'm fit enough to do it, that I can condition my mind to survive on little food, in great heat, in unpleasant conditions, with no companions to assist me. Much can be learned from Park's heady pre-trip declaration that he would 'acquire a name greater than any ever did'. Self-confidence for any difficult or risky endeavour relies largely on the power of imagination, on a person's ability to see the end before the end has come, to see oneself exactly where one would like to be.

And you can never know what will happen. Before my departure to Mali, I told my parents what to do with my things if I didn't come back. It wasn't melodrama; I was quite serious. They're used to hearing that from me, I suppose, as I've said it before other trips, but they still don't get used to my insistence on going anyway. They don't *understand* that insistence, as they expend a lot of energy in not disturbing the routine of their lives with anything new, that lacks a guarantee. And I certainly don't criticize them for that; it is who they are. But I've always found myself unsettled by predictability, routine, comfort; I'm lulled by these things, and bored by them, and then my mind turns in on itself and obsesses about utter minutiae. I need doses of the new before me, the strange, the completely unfamiliar, in order to feel truly alive. This probably started early for me. As a child, I never felt an intrinsic sense of belonging anywhere; I've always been fascinated by those who feel rooted to a place, for whom wanderlust becomes a pathology of the soul. All I know is that my trips allow me to unearth parts of myself that I've long since buried as dead, showing me who I can be. They are, in many respects, processes of rebirth.

I stop paddling to watch a fragile white butterfly beat its way across the Niger, a river that is easily a mile wide. Where does this tiny creature get its energy to pump those wings? It flutters and dives above my kayak, already halfway across the river, another half-mile to go. All around it is the sure death of these silver waters, and no wind to help it along. By what will did it make this crossing? And to what? The greenery on both sides of the Niger looks the same. I hold up the respite of my paddle blade, but it swirls away towards the sun and continues on.

I think of Park, who earned a place in history's annals as one of the most intrepid and craziest explorers that ever lived. He embarked into an unmapped part of the world that existed in the minds of Europeans solely as speculation, myth or hearsay. It was a country known for its hostile peoples and notoriously fatal diseases; if he got into trouble, there would be absolutely no-one to help him. Park's unwavering ambition has always fascinated me. I'm hoping that, by duplicating his journey as best I can, I will come to know what drove him alone into West Africa's interior. Some historians have suggested that he had a death wish or was mad. Others claim he was interested in money or fame. But I suspect that Park possessed an uncanny and insatiable curiosity for the unknown, which was fed all the more by this spectacular country: the verdant shores, the somnolent waters, a sun that dazzles the river with light. Park, a product of Scotland's dreary moors, must have found Mali a blithe country.

In December 1795, he began his first journey to the Niger River from the British river port of Pisania, in modern-day Gambia, in the company of an African man hired as a translator and a Mandingo slave boy, owned by a local British doctor, who had been ordered to accompany him (the doctor had promised the boy his freedom if he and Park ever successfully returned – though the doctor had his doubts). 'I believe,' Park wrote, '[that the doctor and his acquaintances] secretly thought they should never see me afterwards.' Indeed, the Association for the Promotion of the Discovery of Africa – Park's London sponsors – had already sent three explorers on identical quests to try to reach the Niger and Timbuktu, one turning back and two dying in the attempt. Park was their latest hopeful, but the meagre £200 advance they gave him for his transportation costs and supplies suggests they had little faith in him. None of this seemed to faze Park, though, and he headed east along the Gambia River without any knowledge of or experience in Africa, riding across what is now Senegal into Mali, with only his two companions, provisions for a couple of days, tobacco and beads for village bartering, a compass, a sextant, muskets, spare clothing and all the blind, reckless will in the world.

I feel not unlike Park, with my own meagre remuneration promised me from the National Geographic Society if

I should succeed – *if* – and a single backpack in my kayak holding everything that I hope will suffice for my trip. I stop paddling to pump Niger River water into my bottles, dropping the filtration pump's tube into a river rife with raw sewage, marvelling at the clear water coming out the other end. Just to be on the safe side, I plop in a couple of iodine tablets. In such a way, I suppose it could be said that my needs are all met – for at least as long as my turkey jerky holds out.

When Park travelled, local kings kept begging him to turn back, warning that the interior tribes would never have seen a white man or his European goodies. Park, of course, continued. He came across people who had never seen the likes of him but were too afraid to approach. 'Two Negro horsemen,' Park wrote in his narrative,

> armed with muskets, came galloping from among the bushes: on seeing them I made a full stop; the horse-men did the same, and all three of us seemed equally surprised and confounded at this interview. As I approached them their fears increased, and one of them, after casting upon me a look of horror, rode off at full speed; the other, in a panic of fear, put his hand over his eyes, and continued muttering prayers until his horse, seemingly without the rider's knowledge, conveyed him slowly after his companion.

Park's luck would run out when the Moors, a North African Arab people living in parts of Mali, heard about the strange white man. They caught up with Park and robbed him of everything but the clothes on his back, his hat and his compass (thought to be an evil talisman), keeping him prisoner in the deserts of what is now Mauritania. It would become the darkest time of his first journey.

I found this part of his narrative the most poignant. He doesn't hide his distress, and his trademark equanimity fails him, revealing glimpses of a traumatizing ordeal. Many male adventurers of his time chose to avoid such candour, opting instead for bravado or tedious ethnographical digressions. But Park did not want his own suffering or others' to pass without witness. When the Mandingo boy was seized into slavery by the Moors, Park became hopelessly distraught. He had come to care about him like a son. 'I [shook] hands with this unfortunate boy,' Park wrote, 'and blended my tears with his, assuring him, however, that I would do my utmost to redeem him.' The boy would never be seen again. Park was left alone among strangers, kept prisoner in a tent in the Sahara during the most scorching months of the year, enduring dawn-to-dusk taunts from crowds of Moors and a humiliating lack of privacy. At one point a wild hog was tied beside him:

This animal had certainly been placed there by order [of Ali, Park's captor] out of derision to a Christian; and I found it a very disagreeable inmate, as it drew together a number of boys, who amused themselves by beating it with sticks, until they had so irritated the hog that it ran and bit at every person within its reach.

With the returning day commenced the same round of insult and irritation: the boys assembled to beat the hog, and the men and women to plague the Christian.

But Park's grim trip had its moments of comic relief. Moorish women were Park's most frequent visitors. He tells us, 'they asked [me] a thousand questions; inspected every part of my apparel, searched my pockets, and obliged me to unbutton my waistcoat and display the whiteness of my skin: they even counted my toes and fingers, as if they doubted whether I was in truth a human being ... and in this manner I was employed, dressing and undressing, buttoning and unbuttoning, from noon to night.' It turns out that the women were interested in inspecting one part of his anatomy in particular. Park tells of this experience with his usual air of propriety, but it was none the less a passage that shocked and amused his early-nineteenth-century readership: 'A party of [women] came into my hut, and gave me plainly to understand that the object of their visit was to ascertain, by actual inspection, whether the rite of circumcision extended to the Nazarenes (Christians), as well as to the followers of Mahomet.' Park handled the situation deftly, declaring that only the youngest and most beautiful of the women would be allowed an exclusive view. Still, Park tells us that the chosen woman 'did not avail herself of the privilege of inspection'.

The humour is short-lived after that. At one point during Park's captivity, he found himself gravely ill. He entreated the Moors to leave him alone to recuperate, discovering that he had 'solicited in vain: my distress was a matter of sport to them, and they endeavoured to heighten it, by every means in their power. This studied and degrading insolence, to which I was constantly exposed, was one of the bitterest ingredients in the cup of captivity; and often made life itself a burden to me.' The days turned into months. During a wedding party, an old woman threw a bowl of bridal urine in his face. Park was subsequently threatened with death, with the amputation of his right hand, with having his eyes poked out. But somehow the intrepid Scotsman kept his cool, acquiescing to nearly every request, never losing his temper, never getting self-righteous – behaviour which certainly saved his life. Park wrote, 'I readily complied with every command, and patiently bore every insult; but never did any period of my life pass away so heavily: from sunrise to sunset, was I obliged to suffer, with an unruffled countenance.'

Park's trials among the Moors would give him unremitting nightmares for years, long after he launched a brave escape from them in the middle of the night and made his way back to England to write his narrative. I try to imagine Park during this darkest time, spending lonely, fitful nights in confinement in the desert, wondering if the next day would see him losing his eyes, having a hand cut off, being killed in some horrible way. What thoughts about his journey then? What doubts? 'But the man whose soul has been enlightened by his Creator,' Park wrote, 'will look upon the joys and afflictions of this life as equally the tokens of Divine love.' Did Park have the wherewithal to take a step back from his suffering long enough to see it all as part of some grand scheme, as a token of 'Divine love' meant to teach him about the nature of existence? This is for me one of the hardest notions to fathom: that life's most tragic events, its greatest sufferings, unfold with some kind of arcane purpose and design. It shoots anger and sadness through my heart. It troubles my mind with questions.

We do know that Park not only survived his treatment, seizing an opportunity to escape, but that he continued on his quest to find the Niger. He led a skeletal horse through the sandy plains of central Mali, begging for food at villages, escaping from bandits and ill-wishers, nearly dying of thirst. Miraculously, he reached the Niger. He would later be credited with having, in 1797, been the first Western explorer to discover the river, which helped to make his ensuing narrative, *Travels in the Interior Districts of Africa*, a bestseller. Park took care to describe the moment: 'I saw with infinite pleasure the great object of my mission; the long sought for, majestic Niger, glittering to the morning sun, as broad as the Thames at Westminster, and flowing slowly to the *eastward*. I hastened to the brink, and, having drank of the water, lifted up my fervent thanks in prayer, to the Great Ruler of all things, for having thus far crowned my endeavours with success.' But Park's enthusiasm for his discovery miffed the local peoples, who of course had known about the Niger for millennia and had their own name for it – the Joliba, or Great Water. The sight of a bedraggled white man staring at its shores, composing lofty paeans to its name, puzzled them. Park would write of a Bambarra man's reaction: 'When he was told that I had come from a great distance, and through many dangers, to behold the Joliba river, [he] naturally inquired if there were no rivers in my own country, and whether one river was not like another.'

As I travel the river, I wonder if the Bozo or Somono fishermen have the same questions about me. What brings me here? Don't I have rivers closer to home? Why come to their Niger? Most people in these parts will never have been any further than Bamako, if they have been anywhere at all. For them, travelling is undertaken for some sort of pragmatic purpose. They might pole their canoes along to attend a village market, or they might make a longer journey to town to buy some hard-to-find supplies. But to travel the river for the sake of travelling? Now that idea must be strange indeed. And how would I explain it? Certainly, my presence here is the result of growing up in a wealthy society that affords many of its people the chance for such specialized pursuits. I know I come to Mali out of this position, and this fact has always embarrassed me about travelling in developing countries, but has also incited me to try to understand the forces that have denied such a standard of life to the majority of the people I encounter.

The sun begins to fall behind some distant hills. I look out at Park's 'majestic Niger', the soft waters catching the orange of the departing sun. I wonder if such a sight would have been enough reward for the travails he had suffered: loss of all his possessions, brutal confinement by the Moors,

32

half-starved wanderings in the Malian desert. I recall a conversation Park had with a local king: 'I repeated what I had before told [the king] concerning the . . . reasons for passing through his country. He seemed, however, but half-satisfied. The notion of travelling for curiosity was quite new to him. He thought it impossible, he said, that any man in his senses would undertake so dangerous a journey merely to look at the country and its inhabitants.' Before the discovery and use of quinine to cure malaria, travel to West Africa was a virtual death sentence for Europeans, akin to being sent to the Russian Front. Colonial powers used only their most insubordinate and expendable soldiers, many of them petty thieves and criminals, to man the forts and oversee operations on the coast. It wasn't uncommon for expeditions to lose half their men to fever and dysentery, if the natives didn't get them first. So Mungo Park's ambitious plan of heading up the Gambia River, crossing what is now Senegal into Mali, then heading by boat up the Niger River to Timbuktu hadn't a modern-day equivalent. It was beyond gutsy – it was borderline suicidal.

Park's troubles didn't end upon his discovery of the river. Mansong, the king of an area then known as Bambarra, tried to get the destitute white man off his hands by giving him money and encouraging him to get out of town and go back to his own people. Park didn't take the hint. He instead began the first of his two river journeys on the Niger, this one beginning from the site of present-day Old Ségou or Ségou Korro – my own starting point. But,

surprisingly for Park, he gave up this first venture, providing this explanation:

> Worn down by sickness, exhausted by hunger and
> fatigue; half naked, and without any article of value,
> by which I might procure provisions, clothes or
> lodging; I began to reflect seriously on my situation. I
> was now convinced, by painful experience, that the
> obstacles to my further progress were insurmountable
> . . . I had but little hopes of subsisting by charity, in a
> country where the Moors have such influence. But
> above all, I perceived that I was advancing, more and
> more, within the power of those merciless fanatics;
> and . . . I was apprehensive that I should sacrifice my
> life to no purpose; for my discoveries would perish
> with me.

Park made an extraordinary decision for a man so
stubbornly possessed by his journey – he decided to make
the long trip back home. Still, this return was just as
fraught with uncertainty as a trip on the Niger would have
been. But he had no choice. 'Whichever way I turned,' he
wrote, 'nothing appeared but danger and difficulty. I saw
myself in the midst of a vast wilderness, in the depth of the
rainy season; naked and alone; surrounded by savage
animals, and men still more savage. I was five hundred
miles from the nearest European settlement.'

His retreat had barely begun when he was robbed and
assaulted by bandits, who stripped him naked and left him

to die in the desert. And here is the Mungo Park that I seek in my own journey, the man who, during this most desperate of times, when his strength and will all but left him, noticed the beauty of some moss nearby, which he studied with infinite patience and admiration. 'Can that Being,' Park waxed, 'who planted, watered, and brought to perfection, in this obscure part of the world, a thing which appears of so small importance, look with unconcern upon the situation and sufferings of creatures formed after his own image? – surely not! Reflections like these would not allow me to despair. I started up, and disregarding both hunger and fatigue, travelled forwards.'

I can't imagine Park's difficulties. I have only an arm that is swelled and tender to move, each pull of the paddle causing jolts of pain. Such an injury would have never slowed Park down, let alone stopped him. Still, I wish this had occurred a week or two into my trip, not on the first day. Who knows if it will get better – or worse? I rewrap it with an Ace bandage and try to forget about it. Timbuktu or bust.

I find inspiration in the fact that Park weathered his trials, making it back to the coast and safely to England, where he became an instant celebrity with the publication of his book. Still, nine years later he would return to West Africa, to the very country that had nearly killed him. Some historians believe he did it for the money. For all his success, Park never became rich, and his life as a country doctor in Scotland could barely make ends meet. But money troubles were only half the story. Park's venturesome spirit – like the proverbial genie let loose from the bottle – could no longer be contained. Scotland hardly compared to the fantastic world which had thrown open its doors to him. 'I would rather brave Africa and all its horrors,' Park confided to his friend Sir Walter Scott, 'than wear out my life in long and toilsome rides over cold and lonely heaths and gloomy hills, assailed by the wintry tempest, for which the remuneration was hardly enough to keep body and soul together.' Park knew that he possessed a rare ability to survive the worst kinds of adversity in the loneliest quarters of the world – a talent greatly in demand during the British Empire's heyday of colonial acquisition. He saw for himself an opportunity to better his prospects.

Park began petitioning the government for opportunities to lead expeditions abroad, in such places as the untamed lands of New South Wales (now south-eastern Australia). He made visits to London with his requests, writing letters to his wife back in Scotland that were full of love and hope for financial security: 'My lovely Ailie, you are constantly in my thoughts. I am tired of this place, but cannot lose the present opportunity of doing something for our advantage.' His petitions would fail until the British government became interested in Africa again and offered Park an impressive commission: go back to West Africa, to the Niger, reach Timbuktu, and then figure out where the river terminates. This time Park would be lavishly outfitted, and he'd be accompanied by forty-four British soldiers, to be chosen from those posted in forts by the Gambia River. For Park, this venture would not only yield a large financial boon if successful, but would also mean an extraordinary achievement on behalf of God, king and country. Park readily agreed.

I approach a family travelling in a long dug-out canoe — daughter, mother, grandmother, with the young sons and father doing all the paddling. We glide past each other, everyone looking at me with wonder, their hesitant smiles bursting into grins and laughter when I greet them in Bambarra: '*Iniché, somo-go?*' Hello, how is your family?

'*Toro-té, aniché,*' they respond. Fine, thank you.

I took pains to learn some of the basic words and phrases of the languages I'll encounter along the next six hundred miles of the river. Greetings, of course, but also very practical terms: 'Is it close?', 'Far?', 'Here?', 'Over there?', 'Where am I?' and 'I don't understand.' I also learned words for items or animals I might have to buy or eat or, God forbid, avoid: fish, rice, hippo, crocodile. And, of course, I made sure I could say, 'I'm going to Timbuktu!' (Colourfully, in the Songhai language: *Ye koi Tomboctoo!*)

Park must have made similar preparations for his return trip to the Niger in search of Timbuktu and the termination of the river. Presumably he must have also pondered his odds of succeeding, deciding they were in his favour. After all, though alone and wretched on his first journey, he'd still managed to discover the Niger, and so what would forty-four armed soldiers and a king's wealthy sponsorship do for him? The proposed second trip must have seemed laughably easy by comparison to his first journey. Park declared in a proposal to a government minister that his expedition would lead to 'the extension of British commerce and the enlargement of our geographical knowledge'. He was rewarded with a captain's commission, a generous subsidy of £5,000 and all the supplies and pack animals he needed for the journey.

His goals were explicitly outlined to him: he was to travel on the Niger River, visit Timbuktu and ascertain the wealth of the city and its environs, take note of the location of natural resources and prospective trade opportunities, determine the feasibility of European settlement, and find where the Niger terminated. It was this last directive that had been the subject of debate for centuries in Europe: where did the Niger end? Though Europeans had long known about the river, no-one had much information about it. Some believed it joined the Nile. Others were convinced from faulty Greek accounts that it ended in a great inland sea. Still others believed it curved down and merged with the Congo River or actually passed *beneath* the Sahara, emptying into the Mediterranean. But regardless, everyone knew that with the secret of its course lay a means of opening up the African continent to commerce, and in particular a lucrative trade in gold. Discovering the route of the Niger and its mystical Timbuktu could make men rich, could build empires.

And so Park went back for a second helping of the country that had nearly killed him. He left behind a wife and three children, a medical practice, and a fame that might have sustained his ego, if not his pocketbook. He reached the Gambian coast on 28 March 1805, political red tape and assorted other difficulties delaying his departure for the interior; it wasn't until the malarial rainy season that Park was prepared to go, and he vowed to begin regardless of the weather (any further delays might have inflamed his sponsors). In his pre-departure letters he maintained a cheerful attitude, making no reference to the tropical storms and their accompanying illnesses that would soon kill his men by the handful. No mention, either, that his soldiers were some of the poorest examples of military manpower in the British Empire, most of them drunkards, deserters or navy convicts who were pardoned in exchange for accompanying Park on his crazy adventure. Ominously, Park had been unable to bribe or cajole any native recruits into joining him in his venture, a fact that he admitted to one of his superiors back in England: 'No inducement,' Park wrote, 'could prevail on a single Negro to accompany me.' But he didn't openly despair. Surely he understood that any doubts on his part might be seen as a sign of un-acceptable weakness. He had to uphold his reputation as one of Europe's greatest adventurers.

As Park headed towards the Niger, his journey barely under way, the first of a long series of mishaps and mis-fortunes befell him. Soldiers became sick with dysentery, giardia, malaria, yellow fever, and died one after the next. Severe storms further demoralized the remaining men. Natives incessantly robbed the sickly, undefended convoy, stealing animals and cargo. Rivers swelled with rain, men drowning in the attempt to cross. Hostile village chiefs extorted money. Wild animals – lions, crocodiles, hyenas –

attacked the stragglers. Overburdened horses and donkeys died or refused to move. Even killer bees tormented the expedition. It was, in short, an utter disaster.

As I paddle along, night approaches, bringing with it concerns of where I can safely stop and sleep. I scan the banks of the river, not yet ready to break my solitude by pulling into a village for the evening. I can't say how I might be received by the local people, though the fishermen I've encountered have been friendly. One of the most frequently recurring themes in Park's narrative was a similar wariness about how he might be greeted at each new village. As he quickly discovered: you just have to take your chances.

Luck wasn't on Park's side when he made it to the Niger for the second time, forty of his original forty-four soldiers dead, all of his pack animals killed or stolen. It wasn't long before his closest companion on the expedition, a brother-in-law from Scotland, died. A distraught Park recorded the death in his journal, and it is one of the few times he so openly expresses his feelings of despair. Otherwise, he keeps up a masquerade of denial, insisting that he hadn't been affected by 'the smallest gloom' until then. The events described in his journals tell a different story. In nearly every entry, there is only catastrophe. Dying soldiers being left behind. Park constantly backtracking in search of lost donkeys or sickly men. Natives robbing the hapless convoy at every opportunity, becoming bolder and bolder as the men suffered increasing illness. One finds it hard to believe that not 'the smallest gloom' ever overshadowed poor Mungo Park and his operation.

But Park was determined to plug on – perhaps because, in addition to an enormous, irrational aversion to failure, he had also caught the Timbuktu fever of those times, calling the fabled city 'the great object of my search'. Having gone that far, he would rather die than give up his quest.

With all his carpenters dead, he faced the daunting task of constructing a boat to sail on the Niger. At the same time, he was battling severe dysentery. Becoming gravely ill and fearing the failure of his mission, he did something well in tune with his remarkable fortitude – he poisoned his system to the point of near-death. 'As I found that my strength was failing fast,' Park wrote in his journal, 'I resolved to change myself with mercury. I accordingly took calomel till it affected my mouth to such a degree that I could not speak or sleep for six days. The salivation put an immediate stop to the dysentery.' One might wonder why he decided to continue with the journey, given all that had happened to him by this time. Historians speculate that Park had become so deranged by sickness that he couldn't think rationally any more.

Park managed to piece together a couple of rotten canoes, outfitting his 'H.M.S. *Joliba*' with rawhide shields to protect him from hostile tribes downriver. He wrote some final letters – to his wife and his sponsor, Lord Camden. To the latter, he maintained a sense of optimism that was nothing short of extraordinary, given the circumstances: 'I am afraid your lordship will be apt to consider matters as in a very hopeless state, but I assure you

I am far from desponding . . . I shall set sail to the east with the fixed resolution to discover the termination of the Niger or perish in the attempt.' And thus he left the town of Sansanding, never to be seen again.

Of the river journey itself, none of Park's written accounts were recovered, so we can know nothing definitively. There are only the verbal recollections given by a guide and translator he had hired. This man, Amadi Fatouma, described a journey plagued by tragedy, Park refusing to stop or leave his boat, local tribes chasing him in canoes and attacking him. If Fatouma is to be believed, Park had to shoot his way down the Niger. Apparently, Park spurned local kings, who demanded duties from him to pass through their kingdoms, armed men preventing him from landing at the port of Timbuktu. Though there are accounts other than Fatouma's that tell of Park's entering the golden city, we do know for certain that he never made it to the river's termination in the Atlantic Ocean. He drowned or was killed in the rapids of Bussa (in Nigeria), with the truth of where he stopped and what he saw dying with him. Thus began the legend of Mungo Park, the iron-willed adventurer extraordinaire, rumoured to be the first white man ever to reach Timbuktu. At the very least, he was the first to have reached its port.

I float along in my kayak, night settling resolutely upon the river. I pull over, deciding to camp behind some reeds. The Niger's dark waters turn north-east, towards Timbuktu, a city as distant and unimaginable to me now as it must have been to Park, who had only the descriptions in a popular book to go on. Written in 1526 by slave-turned-scholar Leo Africanus, *The History and Description of Africa and the Notable Things Contained Therein* described the city as a veritable El Dorado, a place of higher learning where palaces were steeped in gold. By all estimates, Africanus was not far off the mark. At the time he visited Timbuktu, it remained the height of wealth and haute couture, the pearl of West Africa's great Songhai Empire, home to universities, extensive libraries, Africa's largest and grandest mosque, and a population exceeding fifty thousand people. The city thrived off its remote but convenient location: the pit stop between the great Saharan caravan routes and the Niger River. It was here that men traded salt, painstakingly harvested from the scorching plains of the Sahara, for the gold, ivory and slaves that came from the south. Slavery would become one of Timbuktu's most lucrative operations, the Arabs giving the Niger the name Neel el Abeed, River of Slaves. However, Africanus would insist that the sale of books from Timbuktu was 'more profitable than any other goods'. The Saharan city was to Africa what Florence had been to Enlightenment Europe – a place renowned for its scholarly and artistic endeavours, where learning and culture reached a zenith of sophistication during the Songhai Empire's reign from 1463 to 1591.

But unbeknownst to Europeans, this wealth of Timbuktu disappeared after 1591, when an army of Moors and mercenaries crossed the Sahara with the most sophisticated weaponry of the time – cannon and muskets – and sacked the golden city in a single day. It marked the end of Timbuktu's scholarly and entrepreneurial supremacy, beginning a decline from which the city would never recover. Still, ill-informed Europeans embarked, one after the next, for an African El Dorado that didn't exist any more. There were only two ways to get there, neither very promising: you could risk enslavement or death by trying to cross the great ocean of sand from the north, or brave the malarial jungles of West Africa and then travel up the Niger. Park's journey would usher in the frantic 'Timbuctoo Rush' of the early 1800s, and it wasn't long before the River of Slaves and its surrounding country came to be known as 'the White Man's Grave'.

# CHAPTER TWO

IT'S THE MIDDLE OF THE NIGHT AND I WAKE WITH A start: the bear bell on my kayak is ringing – two men have discovered my boat. From inside my tent pitched on shore, I can hear them whispering to each other, the light from their torch flickering anxiously about the dark shore. I had hoped that the bell would prove an unnecessary – if not paranoid – precaution on my part, but here we are: the middle of the night, two strange men going through my things, and only a can of mace and some martial arts training between me and potential theft and/or bodily harm.

I forget about this sort of thing before I go on these trips. Or, more accurately, I ignore the possibility of this sort of thing happening. It's hard when you don't know a place and its people yet. There are no experts to call because no-one has done this before, no Lonely Planet guides to consult for precautions when camping alone along the Niger. In this case, I don't even know what tribe

I'm dealing with. Fulani or Bambarra? Bozo or Somono? Each has different customs, different points of view. Each wonders why you're here. Usually these issues work themselves out. People tend to be nice and hospitable. Usually. But then my bear bell starts ringing in the middle of the night.

But they don't know that I'm alone. And they don't know that I'm a woman. I could be a big, bad white guy with an attitude. So I get up, arm myself with a section of a kayaking paddle, and burst out of my tent, yelling, '*Hey!*' in a deep, madman's voice.

It works. They flee in their canoe, paddles making a *splunking* sound in the river. I watch in the faint moonlight as they disappear around a bend, sighing in relief, my breath quivering.

But it's not over yet. I hear their voices again. And now I see their flashlight beam coming towards me across the savannah. I run to take down my tent, stuffing things into my kayak wherever they'll fit. In a matter of minutes, I have all my possessions in the boat and shove off. The men reach my camping spot soon after I leave, and they stand on the shore: two dark figures barely distinguishable from the starless night. I paddle hard over the lurid, silver-coloured waters, the river nearly a mile wide here and no telling how deep.

I stop after a while, sitting back in my seat, letting the waves pull and tug at my boat. All around me the lapping, quicksilver waters. No sight of land, no suggestion of people. Like experiencing some sort of primordial beginning of the world, the womb of creation. All I have is my little boat, the air within its cavities keeping me afloat in this void. I'm scared to make a sound, as if even a deep breath might somehow disturb the complex machinations of conception. I might be the last person alive in the world, or the first. That's how it feels right now. The thought makes me uneasy, as does the idea of napping on a West African river in the middle of the night. Not surprisingly, sleep won't come, so I just float along to wherever the river wants to take me, wondering what might have happened if I'd stayed on shore. Unpleasant as it is to be floating like this, and tired as I am, I'm convinced I made the right decision by leaving.

When I was young, I wasn't very prudent about anything. I just didn't know any better. I'd take all these outrageous risks. My mother worked as a waitress late into the night, while my father – in his own unfathomable world of depression – sat in his spot on the sofa after work and barely moved or spoke until bedtime. I was left to do whatever I wanted. And I did. Went to places where little girls probably shouldn't have gone. I collected cans at forest preserves for spare change, wandering in the midst of motorcycle gangs having parties, black-leathered folk who shared their beers with me. Budweiser, usually. I raided the dumpsters behind porn shops with my brother, biking off with my booty to sell it to neighbourhood boys. Got in fights with those same boys, with lots of boys, gained a reputation for kicking their asses. It was the classic acting-out of childhood, if I look behind all the messiness of past events. Just a desperate need for attention and love that, when unfulfilled, has a way of evolving into fierce independence, tenacity, a drive to take care of oneself at all costs.

Do they stay with us, those old needs? Are they the mysterious source of wanderlust, the secret ache propelling all journeys? It's tempting to draw too quick a conclusion. Mungo Park was said to be notoriously reserved, a dreamer and lover of romantic poetry. His mind was filled with Scottish ballads, tales of daring, hardship, perseverance. His father wanted him to become a minister, but he chose medicine instead. Those were the days of bleedings with leeches, of using poison to cure. Park adapted himself well to this work, but found his interests veered elsewhere, to botany. He obtained a position as surgeon for the East India Company and was soon off to Sumatra, where he busied himself with classifying plants and animals that he found in the jungle. He returned to Scotland after a year, the travel bug having bitten him. He was hopelessly lost in the fantastic worlds he had found, regardless of the dangers they might hold.

I get similarly lost in what's out there; every few months I'm hungry for a journey. But I have trouble explaining this to some people. I remember my flight from Paris to Mali. I was sitting next to a Frenchman named Jean who was travelling to Bamako on business. He wore a short-sleeved pastel blue shirt and dress pants, which he was anxiously patting and pulling at as if it were a costume he couldn't wait to take off. He kept smoothing back the greying hair at his temples, gazing through his glasses at the map of the Niger River in my lap. I could see that he'd been wondering about me. And with our flight from Paris nearly over, Mali's capital Bamako approaching, he leaned back and turned to me, his voice jarring the silence.

'Are you in the Peace Corps?' he asked. Which is, apparently, the only reason why any Americans go to Mali.

I shook my head. 'I'm going to be travelling on the Niger River,' I said. 'In a kayak.'

'A kayak?' He sputtered his lips. 'Where will you go?'

'I'm paddling from Ségou to Timbuktu.'

'That's very far!'

'Well, it's about six hundred miles,' I said.

'Will you go alone?'

I nodded.

'Do you know someone who has done this before?' he asked.

'No. As far as I know, I'll be the first.'

And Jean felt compelled to lean across the aisle and tell his friend, who looked at me and grinned as he heard the translation in French.

'There are no hotels in the country. When you leave Bamako, there is nothing,' his friend said to me. He emphasized the word 'nothing' as if we were back in Mungo Park's time, as if he were speaking about great unknown spaces, Darkest Africa.

'Yeah, I know. I'll be camping,' I tell him.

'Camping? But lions!' Jean said.

'I'll also be staying in villages.'

'And hippos,' his friend added. 'There are hippos in the river, and they are very dangerous. Do you know this?'

Hippos I knew about. As a matter of fact, I had a strange, irrational fear of hippos that was so strong it might have come out of a past life. Before my trip, fearing these creatures more than anything else, I called some well-known travel writers, names given to me by the magazine, men in their fifties or sixties who had been everywhere on the globe by now, several times over. What about hippos? I asked them. What does one do about hippos?

They hadn't any suggestions for me. They'd never kayaked through hippo country, and they advised me not to do it either. They advised me about other things, too. 'Look,' one person said to me, 'you don't want to do this trip without having someone on the ground to tell you what's out there. You need to find out if a village up ahead is going to kill you for your camera.' Which was a very different kind of paternal advice from what my father used to give me when I was growing up – 'Lock the door when you leave.'

'I'll deal with hippos when they come,' I said to the Frenchman.

'Do you think these villages will be safe?' Jean asked.

'I don't know,' I said. 'Hopefully.'

Days before I was supposed to leave, my travel doctor handed me a memo from the US State Department about Mali. Parts of it stood out to me:

female travelers, in particular, have reported being harassed. Travelers should stay alert, remain in groups, and avoid poorly lit areas after dark. Corruption is prevalent. Poorly maintained, over-loaded transport and cargo vehicles frequently break down and cause accidents. Undisciplined drivers render traffic movements unpredictable. Nighttime driving is particularly hazardous as vehicles lack headlights and/or taillights. Safety of public trans-portation: poor. Availability of roadside assistance: poor. Avoid traveling on Air Mali due to safety concerns. Visitors should not travel overland to the northern regions. Banditry is a serious risk. Travel should be avoided on the left bank of the Niger River and outside major centers.

I anticipated having to break several of those rules, if not all of them. There seemed to be no way of avoiding it. Most obviously, I would definitely need to land on the dreaded left bank of the Niger River, and of course my entire trip was predicated on venturing 'outside major centers'. Without specific literature, or the advice from famous travel writers who had been there and done that, what I was about to do was merely a blank screen to put my experiences on. And while I felt fear, I didn't let it become my modus operandi, ruling my life and decisions to the point of immobility. This is the trade-off that I have acknowledged and accepted for my life: I am willing to sacrifice some of my security for the excitement of raw adventure. Which means, of course, that I must be prepared to accept all consequences. And which also means, generally, that my trips have large helpings of the unpleasant side of things.

Fear of danger is a funny thing, too. It tends not to be around when it ought to be; it definitely has an agenda of its own. It's ironic how danger doesn't present itself when we'd expect, but instead creeps and connives to appear when we feel the most safe. Before I left on this trip, I was at a Buddhist retreat in rural north-western Missouri. This was a place of sunny cornfields, of spicy country air smelling of goldenrod and milkweed. I stayed at a Benedictine monastery, brown-robed monks silently wandering the grounds, used to all of us weird Buddhist and tai-chi folk who moved around like zombies outside. You rarely heard the sound of cars there, and the sun set each night in pale red hues over fields that sent armies of fireflies whirling into the dusk. It felt like the safest place I had ever been, which was saying a lot, as I had visited war zones and killing fields and been in the midst of a coup, and I had come to believe that every place is draped in horror, either latent or realized. But here was a place where the front gate hadn't been locked in fifty years, where men prayed over meals and sang hymns of faith and love each night.

Shortly after I left, a lone man, armed with rifles and ammunition, drove through the gate of the monastery. The evening news showed that he parked in the same spot where I had parked, walked casually into the monastery, and fired at everyone he saw. He critically injured two monks and killed another two before walking into the chapel and sitting in the pew where I had sat, no doubt staring at the same painting of Jesus that I had seen, and blowing his brains out.

No place is safe. Safety itself is an illusion. And I wonder if it is my deep acceptance of this that makes it easier for me to do these trips. No place is safe. And while I don't advocate tempting fate, I guess I just don't worry much about it either.

I remember how on that plane with Jean, it was dark and raining outside. We descended towards Bamako through thick stormclouds that gave only a shady, fretful view of the landscape below. Jean was holding his head as the plane dipped and rose, letting out soft moans. I didn't see many lights on the ground, nor were there neat displays of houses, or skyscrapers, or highways, or anything familiar. Just a nervous darkness without shape or form. Even the runway appeared like a clumsy trail of lights that strained to be seen through rain and shadow. I felt my heart leap along with the struggling plane, feeling twinges of regret. But it was too late. The journey had caught me, from the minute I got on the plane, and it would take me to whatever end.

I turned to Jean, wanting to keep things light-hearted. 'So, do you like Mali?' I asked. He was still holding his head in his hands. Our plane carefully visited the runway only to peel into the air at the last minute, to try again.

He sighed and looked at me incredulously. 'I prefer France,' he said.

*

I sit up in my kayak now. A large canoe is coming directly towards me from the darkness. I take up my paddle and drive myself away, nearly hitting it, and look back to see no-one inside. Like a canoe driven by ghosts, the large black vessel disappearing into the moonlight.

I hear the sound of waves now – I seem to be entering some kind of rapid. I secure my things and paddle towards the opposite shore where I see a distant light, not wanting to be on this river any more when it's dark out. The waves get bigger, barrelling at me from the darkness. My kayak hits them head-on, spray showering over me. I know I need to get out of the middle of this immense river, yet I can barely see what I'm facing in front of me. I free my flashlight from my bag and hold it in my teeth as I paddle. *Got to get to the shore, to that light*. The waves keep coming at me, drenching me, the current tugging at my rudder and trying to take control of my boat.

I paddle with all the energy I have left, my injured arm screaming in pain. The light on the shore barely seems to get closer. It is the optical illusion of night paddling, the appearance of things as not moving, not getting any closer. I tug even harder at the paddle. And now, at last – it comes closer. And closer still. But what a long night. I'm ready to collapse.

I cut through the fast current and pull towards shore, where I see a dock illuminated by the feeble glow of a kerosene lamp beside a hut. I tie up my kayak, relieved to have arrived safely. A village sleeps near by; my watch reads 4.12 a.m. I pull myself on to shore, grateful for the solid ground beneath me. Lying down, I wrap my rain poncho around me. I don't care what people are going to think when they wake up and see me like this – I'm too tired to worry about it.

Now is the time when my mind asks what I'm doing here, and why this journey. But such thoughts feel insidious, my injured arm swollen and throbbing, mosquitoes trying to find entry to my skin. I close my eyes to try to sleep.

# CHAPTER THREE

I STILL FEEL THE NIGHT IN MY MIND, A HEAVINESS THAT fills my whole body and brings a slow labour to my paddle strokes. The Niger is like a sheet of silk around me, the water soft and pliant before even the slightest movement. The shores look verdant and jungle-like, ringing with the sharp, fervent insect calls left over from the night. I watch the sun rising, its clean white light pressing through morning clouds and filling me with peace.

Something is strange and striking about my time on the river now, and it takes me a few moments to figure out what: there are no signs of Western civilization on the shores. No electrical wires, no phone lines, no roads, no cars. No sounds of engines or of planes overhead. The buildings are constructed from earth and thatch, rather than cement, brick, steel. I see only adobe or woven grass mats wherever there are people. And no hotels, restaurants, gas stations, flushing toilets, running water. No electricity whatsoever, or telephones. I couldn't contact anyone even if I wanted to, nor could anyone find me. This must be what is meant by being 'on my own'. This is what is tantalizing me most about this trip: the necessity of revamping all my requirements and expectations for life, of doing without, of knowing that I need very little to sustain me.

It all amazes me – not a single familiar sight is to be found anywhere along this river. People haul produce as they did thousands of years ago: by donkey cart. They still travel the river in wooden canoes. Motorized boats are entirely absent from the water, with the rare exception of a passing river barge every few days. No-one can afford either the outboard or the petrol, let alone the boat, which particularly surprises me – back home, the waterways are filled with people in their own motorboats, who stream by in a display of noise and diesel exhaust. But none of that here, which is why I feel the odd sensation of going back in time.

My experience on the Niger is probably closer to Mungo Park's first journey here than I ever realized. As I float along in my kayak, I pull out his narrative and read some of the passages, having the bizarre feeling of knowing exactly what he's talking about, of experiencing exactly the same thing, so that two hundred years might have never transpired between our voyages. In one part of his narrative, he wrote about the very country I pass through now:

> We arrived at Modiboo, a delightful village on the banks of the Niger, commanding a view of the river

for many miles, both to the east and west. The small green islands (the peaceful retreat of some industrious Foulahs [Fulani], whose cattle are here secure from the depredations of wild beasts), and the majestic breadth of the river, which is here much larger than at Ségou, render the situation one of the most enchanting in the world. Here are caught great plenty of fish, by means of long cotton nets, which the natives make themselves.

I have seen those very nets, have seen the catches of fish, the lush islands used as safe grazing grounds. I feel closer to the explorer than I ever thought possible.

Waving at the people I meet becomes a pastime now, has moved from novelty to habit. Back home in Missouri, people don't usually wave at each other. They've forgotten how to do it, or perhaps were never taught. Here, it is perpetual greeting and exchanges of good will. And such smiles: the smallest babies transfixed with pleasure to see me in my boat, children whooping and laughing on shore, women grinning. I notice how different we look from each other: I, in my long patterned skirt, my blonde hair and T-shirt and my Australian bush hat; they in their colourful *pagnes*, breasts bared, hair in elaborate cornrows woven with rings of pure gold. But as we stare at each other, the differences dissolve. Beyond the confines of sight, there is no division. We share all those things that make us uniquely human – the joys and pains, loss and hope.

The sun rises and clears away the morning mists. I find

a wide patch of river with barely a current and sit low in my kayak to try to sleep, feeling no fear – the people here are too gentle to hurt anyone. I wake with a start; I must have been drifting for some time. I forget for a moment where I am and look out at the silver waters, seeing my red kayak beneath me. In my dreaming I'd been elsewhere, in some other unimaginable place. For a moment I have to force the world of Mali into my consciousness. All worlds, it seems, are relative.

I paddle past Somono and Bozo fishing villages. Many of the people in these parts believe in a god of the Niger, and they think it's blasphemous to paddle at night without propitiating him. If so, might that explain my difficulties of last night? Sometimes I like to indulge in these ideas of genies and ghosts, wrathful gods and sorcery. *What if?* I imagine a world ordered by another, intangible realm, with everything I do aided or thwarted by forces I can't see. That is a fascinating kind of world to me; I imagine myself as the proverbial pawn in the hand of some greater intelligence, none of the moves my own. The god of the river might toss me in the waves of the Niger, plunge me through storms and rapids, send men after me in the night. I have no say in any of it. This reminds me that far away from Mali's animist roots, in the Far East, many people believe there are no gods. Everything is the result of causes and conditions. Karma. The lives we live and don't live. The things that happen to us in each moment. The kindness and the sufferings we receive. In this sense, there are no accidents or mistakes. Which I find myself rebelling against. I *want* to know that I play some role in outcomes; I *want* to believe that I'm able to dictate where I'm going and what will happen to me. My mind struggles against submitting wholly to the whims of this journey.

As the noonday heat and humidity rise into the mid-90s, according to my thermometer, I keep looking around the next bend for the town of Markala and its incongruous bridge stretching over the Niger – the only such bridge I'll pass all the way to Timbuktu. I feel as if I barely cover any ground, the current so slow and the paddling so long, though I know that impatience is senseless on this trip. I'll get there when I get there. I remind myself that it was this exact stretch of river, during the same season of the year, that had tormented Mungo Park with its heat. 'The canoes were not covered with mats,' he wrote, 'and there being no wind, the sun became insufferably hot. I felt myself affected with a violent headache, which increased to such a degree as to make me almost delirious. I never felt so hot a day; there was sensible heat sufficient to have roasted a sirloin.' Through even the highest SPF sunscreen, I can see my skin turning red and parched. I've been wearing a skirt over a pair of kayaking shorts, which I pull down whenever canoes approach (women who wear pants in rural Mali – let alone shorts – are viewed as prostitutes), and now I'm glad I have the skirt to protect my legs as well. Like Park, I can find no escape from this sun.

The bridge appears in the distance, a long steel structure left over from French colonial days; it looks like something aliens might have dropped into the Malian countryside on a whim. Donkey carts loaded with hay travel across its anachronistic metal rungs; women hang up washing on its girders. The current is so slow that the bridge is a very long time coming. When I do finally pass beneath it – my first clear sign of progress achieved – the Niger begins a 180-degree turn west that will circle northeast again. But progress is short-lived out here. For every landmark I get to, there's always the next one, annoyingly distant. And so frustration and impatience set in. I am a student of impatience; I have a hard time waiting for anything. Back home, when working on projects, all I see is the distance I have to go to reach the end; no progress I make ever seems adequate. Here, though, I can only paddle so fast, and river and weather have an agenda of their own. This journey doesn't care what I want to accomplish.

I'm reminded of the story about the opening of Pandora's box, how the last pestilence about to leave and assail the world was Hope. It is a true human curse – that dogged insistence that things go our way. I must stop estimating how far I'll be able to paddle in a single day. My map, when I look at it, must be only for orienting myself. No plans any more. No objectives other than getting to Timbuktu. I must learn how to stop imposing my demands on the world.

The sun is starting to set; I'll soon be arriving at Sansanding. My injured right arm is so swollen and painful that paddling has turned into an act of masochism, but doctors and hospitals are two more things that don't exist on this river. I put on a wrist brace I brought from home and try to forget about it.

I can feel my excitement rising at the prospect of seeing Sansanding for the first time. This town is almost as special to me as Timbuktu, because Mungo Park was there. He writes about Sansanding in the narratives from both his journeys, and so it feels the closest I'll be able to get to the explorer. In Sansanding, I can actually walk where Park walked, knowing with certainty that our two journeys have finally, undeniably, intersected.

As I pass around the final bend, heading due east, I see Sansanding for the first time. The town looks like some vision from a Coleridge poem. It sits far across a sandy floodplain, the white minarets of one of its mosques rising like castle turrets above the heat waves. I feel further from home than I have ever felt before. I feel like one of the explorers of old, coming upon some secret desert kingdom. As I get closer, I see a collection of brown adobe houses crouching around the great white mosque. Giant, gnarly kapok trees spread branches over the terraced homes. I see a clearing in the middle of the town, filled with empty market stalls. On a high bank sits a graveyard, each plot marked by a tombstone and a flat rock spread on the ground, the graves all facing Mecca. Wooden canoes with pointy ends rest along the shore, where crowds of naked kids play in the water and women do their washing. Everything looks ancient and full of mystery. Here is the epitome of travel to me: being dazed by newness and exoticism, with all previous experience, all former reference points, deserting me utterly.

I paddle round a small bend, approaching Sansanding. The naked children playing in the water spot me and start screaming and jumping around. Women, naked from the waist up and bent over their washing, straighten and gape at me. I wave and say the Bambarra word for hello, *iniché*, and there follows a moment for processing: a lone white woman in a tiny red boat, speaking their language. All at once, they wave enthusiastically to me, and soon well over a hundred people crowd along the shore to await my arrival.

I find it a very unsettling thing to paddle my kayak straight into a crowd so large, so full of excited, yelling, gesticulating people. I have no way of knowing what to expect. Will they greet me warmly? Will they try to pull me from my boat? This town probably never receives tourists. Even the sages at Lonely Planet have failed to give it a sentence or two of mention in their *West Africa* guidebook.

I coast to shore, the rudder scraping on the sandy bottom and lodging me a few feet from dry ground. The crowd surrounds me, with kids squeezing forward to touch my kayak. They reach out their hands tentatively, as if the boat might blow up in their faces. I have never been in the midst of such a big, tight mass of people. I look at them and see fear, shyness, excitement in their faces. I greet them in French and then in Bambarra, and they smile to hear their own language spoken.

'Where are you going, miss?' one man asks me in French.

'To Timbuktu.'

'In this boat?' He steps forward to survey it, squeezing the hull with his hand and holding my paddle. 'That's not possible,' he concludes.

He translates to everyone what I told him, that I intend to paddle all the way to Timbuktu in what he considers a pathetic sham of a boat, and the women touch fingertips to foreheads, muttering, '*Eh, Allah.*'

I try to get out of the boat, but the kids are too thick around me. They press against the kayak, fighting with each other to have the privilege of touching the shiny red skin of the hull. Finally, fortunately, a man with a wooden switch comes forward and drives them away, and I'm able to get out of my kayak.

My experience here is nearly identical to Mungo Park's. 'We reached Sansanding at ten o'clock,' he wrote. 'Such crowds of people came to shore to see us, that we could not land our baggage till the people were beaten away with sticks.' Ironically, Park chose Sansanding for the official start of his second trip because he believed it would offer him a respite from the gaping crowds at Old Ségou. But Sansanding would prove just as troublesome.

Park described his first trip here in his narrative *Travels in the Interior Districts of Africa*, and the experience had been anything but pleasant. Sansanding in 1797 was one of the Niger River's premier slave-trading destinations, inhabited by Moors and black African traders. Even back then, Sansanding was a large place, with roughly nine thousand inhabitants. Park had been the first European to ever set foot there, and had subsequently been the source of much curiosity and alarm. At that time, too, Park was nearly destitute, had only the five thousand cowrie shells (used as money in these parts) that Mansong, King of Bambarra, had given him in an attempt to get the cumbersome white man to leave Ségou. Consequently, Park found himself entirely dependent on native hospitality.

For me, it is much the same scenario, except that I'm not destitute as I have National Geographic Society expense money. I must still find someone willing to put me up for the night. I decide to do what Park did. He had learned to follow the local custom of finding the chief of the town, giving him a large gift, and asking him for permission to lodge in town. I'm a bit wary of trying this myself, though, as Park's first experience here had been anything but agreeable:

I was surrounded with hundreds of people, speaking a variety of different dialects, all equally unintelligible to me. The Moors now assembled in great number; with their usual arrogance, compelling the Negroes to stand at a distance. They immediately began to question me concerning my religion [insisting that] I must conform so far as to repeat the Mahomedan prayers; and when I attempted to waive the subject, by telling them that I could not speak Arabic, one of them ... started up and swore by the Prophet, that if I refused to go to the mosque, he would be the one that would assist in carrying me thither. They compelled me to ascend a high seat, by the door of the mosque, in order that every body might see me; for the people had assembled in such numbers as to be quite ungovernable; climbing upon the houses, and squeezing each other, like the spectators at an execution. Upon this seat I remained until sunset.

*Poor Mungo*, I thought when I read that passage, and I think it now as I try to manoeuvre through the pressing, jostling crowd in search of the *doogootigi*, or chief.

Park's second visit to Sansanding saw him less destitute, but surely more despondent. This was where he spent weeks with the last of his original forty-four soldiers, trying to get some canoes from Mansong so that he could fashion himself a boat for travel down the Niger. I can already imagine what it was like for him: the weeks of wiping sweat from his face and pounding and sanding away, while crowds of naked children stood at arm's length, watching, having no place to go and nothing better to do. Park would have provided unrelenting entertainment for the town's citizens; I wonder if villages had even identified a particular year in their history: the Coming of the Crazy White Man. In fact, European travellers coming after him discovered that Park's name had made it into the songs and oral history of these parts. The words to one such song, sung by a group of women with whom Park had stayed in Old Ségou, went as follows:

*The winds roared, and the rains fell.*
*The poor white man, faint and weary, came and sat under our tree.*
*He has no mother to bring him milk; no wife to grind his corn.*
*Let us pity the white man; no mother has he.*

On his second journey, Park actually intended to reach the termination of the Niger itself (well over a thousand miles from Sansanding), so he needed to make sure his boat was strong, functional and fully equipped with supplies. This careful attention to construction and outfitting took so much time that his few remaining soldiers started to die off from illness, and, though he was personally opposed to slavery, Park saw no choice but to buy a few slaves to help man his boat.

Slavery is a touchy subject in Park's narrative. At the time he left on his trips, England had not yet abolished slavery (which wouldn't happen until 1807) and was still a major participant in the transatlantic trade in human lives, which was one of the most profitable activities a person could be engaged in. A single British ship could expect to earn the equivalent of $100,000 in pounds sterling per shipment of slaves – an unimaginably enormous sum at that time. Still, British abolitionists made headway in the political debate much sooner than their American counterparts, and the trade was becoming less and less acceptable in England. Park found himself writing his narrative at a time when tempers were high on both sides of the debate, and perhaps for this reason he never openly denounced the slave trade in his writing, a fact that has angered some modern critics of his work. But biographers have suggested that Park probably wrote anti-slavery comments in his narrative's original draft, only to have the parts cut out or changed by editors more concerned about profits than principle: criticizing the slave trade would have hurt book sales. It is entirely possible, too, that Park, badly wanting a commission from the British government for a new expedition, decided it wasn't in his best interests to make political enemies.

As Park would point out, West Africa had enjoyed a long tradition of slavery, the institution firmly established in all the regions he travelled through. Park estimated that 'persons of free condition ... constitute, I suppose, not more than one-fourth part of the inhabitants at large; the other three-fourths are in a state of hopeless and hereditary slavery; and are employed in cultivating the land, in the care of cattle, and in servile offices of all kinds, much in the same manner as the slaves of the West Indies'. The Arab and European slave trades greatly exacerbated the problem by providing local slave traders with the most lucrative and unquenchable market for slaves yet, millions of black Africans being shipped to North African and Middle Eastern harems, as well as to the Americas along the infamous Middle Passage. The European hunger for slaves was so great that West Africans widely believed that the white men considered African people a delicacy, and were shipping them away in order to eat them. Park wrote, '[The slaves] repeatedly asked if my countrymen were cannibals. They were very desirous to know what became of the slaves after they had crossed the salt water. [It] is a deeply rooted idea that the whites purchase Negroes for the purpose of devouring them.'

To this day, *de facto* slavery still exists in Mali, up in the north around Timbuktu. Malian officials and anthropologists often deny this, though, saying that slavery was officially abolished. Still, thousands of people – black African Bella people – work for Arab masters as unpaid labourers, unable to end their servitude for myriad economic, social and psychological reasons. If and when I get to Timbuktu, I will find out the truth for myself. I carry two gold coins from home, thinking I might try to free someone with them.

It's impossible for me to view these ancient streets of Sansanding without imagining the thousands of slaves who passed through on their way to the West African coast and European ships. When Park was here, slavery seemed to have reached its height, a fact that thoroughly disgusted him. Though his narrative tries to be politically inoffensive, Park still goes out of his way to describe the brutality of the trade, openly sympathizing with the plight of the enslaved people he encounters on his journeys. Penniless and trying to return to the coast at the end of his first journey, Park accepted the invitation to travel with a slave caravan, or 'coffle' as they were called, for the security it would provide him from bandits. In one chapter, he described at length the fate of a woman slave with whom he had journeyed:

The woman slave ... whose name was Nealee, was not come up [and] they found [her] lying by the rivulet. She was very much exhausted, [refusing] to proceed any farther; declaring that she would rather die than walk another step. As entreaties and threats were used in vain, the whip was at length applied. Though she was unable to rise, the whip was a second time applied, but without effect; upon which Karfa [the leader of the coffle] desired two of the slatees [slavers] to place her upon the ass which carried our dry provisions [and] the woman was carried forward until dark. At daybreak poor Nealee was awakened; but her limbs were now become so stiff and painful, that she could neither walk nor stand; she was therefore lifted, like a corpse, upon the back of the ass. She was quickly thrown off, and had one of her legs much bruised. Every attempt to carry her forward being thus found ineffectual, the general cry of the coffle was, *kang-teri, kang-teri*, 'cut her throat, cut her throat'; an operation I did not wish to see performed, and therefore marched onwards with the foremost of the coffle. The sad fate of this wretched woman made a strong impression.

Park reached the coast with this slave coffle, concerned about the fate of the slaves with whom he had travelled so far and so long. He wrote:

Although I was now approaching the end of my tedious and toilsome journey, and expected, in another day, to meet with countrymen and friends, I could not part, for the last time, with my unfortunate fellow-travellers, doomed, as I knew most of them to be, to a life of captivity and slavery in a foreign land, without great emotion. These poor slaves, amidst their own infinitely greater sufferings, would commiserate mine; and frequently, of their own accord, bring water to quench my thirst, and at night collect branches and leaves to prepare me a bed in the Wilderness. We parted with reciprocal expressions of regret and benediction. My good wishes and prayers were all I could bestow upon them; and it afforded me some consolation to be told, that they were sensible I had no more to give.

This is the Mungo Park I'm searching for on this journey, the man I so often admire. And pity.

I ask the crowd in clunky Bambarra where I might find the chief. A man leads me up some clay steps towards a terraced courtyard. The town is built on a high bank, with winding layers of adobe homes creating narrow, rising passageways. It occurs to me that I've arrived in a less than presentable state: muddy clothes, red and perspiring face, filthy sandals held together with plastic ties, my Australian bush hat collapsed at a strange angle upon my head. I take off my hat and smooth down my hair, wiping mud from my T-shirt. I haven't been travelling by myself long enough to shed the burden of worrying about another's gaze.

I'm led in front of an older man wearing a long, pink robe that reaches his knees, called a *grand bubu* in Mali, with baggy pants and matching pink fez. He lounges on a mat in the shade of a large tree, watching me with displeasure. I straighten my skirt, which sits lopsided over my kayaking shorts, and greet him.

'This is the chief,' a young man who speaks French tells me. 'His name is Badulai.'

The chief frowns at me, swatting flies from his face and fondling a string of prayer beads. Suddenly, he speaks imperiously to me in Bambarra. The entourage around him studies me closely, and the man with the French steps forward.

'The chief wants a gift from you,' he tells me.

'Right.' I had known this request would come, though I wasn't sure at what point during the interview. *Give out the bucks as soon as possible*, I note to myself, as I stick a hand down my skirt into a pocket of my shorts. The chief is frowning and turning his head away, as if I were doing something dirty. I pull out a bill and give it to him. It is a large bill, a generous sum by Malian standards, and the chief seems pleased, his frown receding into a light scowl. Being a chief in these villages is a hereditary honour; I don't see anything further qualifying them. I ask him if I can spend the night in Sansanding, and he nods, telling a man to guide me to the place where I can stay.

They put me up with the town English teacher, Yaya Fomba, a man whose English is so poor that I can barely understand him. I frequently look to his young wife, Yakiri, for French translations. Yakiri is about half Yaya's age, was a former pupil of his. I can see why Yaya was attracted to her – she is robust, attractive, has the kind of wide, benevolent smile that makes you feel immediately at ease. She wears a colourful red-patterned *pagne*, her hair wrapped up in cloth of the same colour. Even the casual dress of women in Mali shows great attention to fashion and elegance, and I feel self-consciously grubby in my sweat-stained T-shirt and wet skirt.

When Yaya hears I'm paddling to Timbuktu, he loses his English for a moment. '*Incroyable*,' he says. Unbelievable.

Yakiri shakes her head and sighs. '*Eh, Allah*,' she says. 'You are crazy! Take the bus.'

We laugh. I rub my injured arm, unable to lift anything with it. Crazy indeed, to be at the beginning of such a long trip with a problematic injury. But I'm as averse to quitting as Park was. I'm determined to get to Timbuktu.

I leave Yaya's house to take a look around Sansanding, trying to find the mosque where Park was on display for the crowds. The dirt streets send up mini-tornadoes of dust and garbage every time the wind blows through town. There is the robust smell of wood ash, the acrid sweetness of decaying fruit and garbage. White doves alight on the mud-brick houses, sidestepping past lizards and bobbing on the edges of the roofs, watching me. I pass the town garbage dump, a deep crater where skeletal donkeys and goats scavenge for scraps. Hens walk in stilted deliberation through the refuse, heads nodding, packs of frantic chicks stumbling in their wake. Adobe homes have grown up around the dump, circling to its very edges, little naked kids playing on the fringe. Sansanding, I've been told by

Yaya, is a prosperous town. I'm wondering what a not-so-prosperous town would look like.

I pass some sheep tied to a tree and stop to touch their noses. The children nearby stare at me and giggle: sheep aren't for petting; they're for eating. I head towards the market, where Mungo traded away the last of his European goods for provisions for his final journey on the Niger. The wooden stalls lie empty though overrun with the omnipresent donkeys and goats, but from the area's sheer size, I can tell it's a hectic place on market day – and has been ever since Park's time. 'The market is crowded with people from morning to night,' he wrote. 'Some of the stalls contain nothing but beads; others indigo in balls; others wood-ashes. In houses fronting the square scarlet and amber silks from Morocco are sold, and tobacco, which comes by way of Timbuctoo. Adjoining this is the salt market, part of which occupies one corner of the square. A slab of salt is sold commonly for eight thousand cowries.' Salt is still valuable, is sold in Malian markets in the shape of large grey slabs that resemble tombstones. It all reminds me that what I find most interesting about a place and its history are not the things that have changed, but what's remained the same.

During one of his lonely, crowd-infested days in the market of Sansanding, Park experienced the greatest blow to his spirits: the death of Alexander Anderson, his brother-in-law and good friend who had accompanied him all the way from Scotland. Park noted the death in his journal:

74

My dear friend Mr Alexander Anderson died after a sickness of four months. I feel much inclined to speak of his merits; but as his worth was known only to a few friends, I will rather cherish his memory in silence, and imitate his cool and steady conduct, than weary my friends with a panegyric in which they cannot be supposed to join. I shall only observe that no event which took place during the journey ever threw the smallest gloom over my mind, till I laid Mr Anderson in the grave. I then felt myself as if left a second time lonely and friendless amidst the wilds of Africa.

I look up and down the shore, wondering if Anderson had been buried beneath these sandy banks, or up in the cemetery beneath the ancient trees. Park must have chosen a good spot for him, out of the sun.

I catch sight of a small mosque nearby, and I go to see how old it is, to see if it could be the one where Mungo Park was surrounded by the crowds. I see a young man by the gate, wearing a long white shirt and embroidered fez. I ask him if I can come inside the gate to look at the mosque.

'No, no,' he says. 'You are a *tubab* – a white person.' He shakes his head and laughs with such amusement that I feel as if I've missed the punchline of some joke. 'It's forbidden for you.'

He tells his friends about my request, as if it were the most outrageous thing he'd ever heard. They all laugh uproariously.

'*C'est interdit*,' one of his friends chimes in. 'Not allowed. You are white.'

Like being excluded from some little boys' playhouse.

I go to visit the other mosque, the largest one with the high white minarets that seems to be the oldest in Sansanding. It's right on the edge of town, facing the river. The caretaker tells me that this mosque was built in 1766, and I get a feeling that it's the right one – Mungo's mosque. I imagine him sitting in its shade with the crowds all around him, gaping at him with his red hair and European dress. For me, fortunately, only small crowds gather. Women with babies wrapped in cotton cloth, slung on their backs. Little boys sporting mohawks: the haircuts mean they've been named after a particular Muslim saint.

'Hey, Mungo,' I say to the mosque. The doves on its roof bob fitfully. 'Mun-go.'

I don't ask if I can go inside the gate.

# CHAPTER FOUR

MY DAYS ARE FILLED NOW WITH THE SLOW PROGRESSION of one passed village after the next, one outcropping of palm trees after another to break up the monotony of sand and shore. At each village the people greet me with waves and exclamations, and I've never met friendlier folk in my life. The women in particular cheer me on, yelling out accolades for '*les femmes fortes*', strong women, which surprises and delights me. Malian women are themselves an underclass, relegated to purely domestic pursuits, 70 per cent of them illiterate. According to various health organizations, at least 90 per cent of them have their clitoris and external genitalia completely removed by the time they're teenagers – one of the highest rates in the world.

It is a cottage industry here, clitoridectomy, as well as excision (removal of the labia) and infibulation (complete removal of all external genitalia and the sewing up of the vaginal opening except for a tiny hole the size of a match head through which the girl must urinate and menstruate). The procedure is generally done by a specially appointed person in the village, who, under typically unsanitary conditions, uses a razor blade or other sharp object to slice off and completely scrape away all of the girl's external genitalia and clitoris. There is no anaesthesia, so the writhing girl must be held down by several adults. When the procedure is finished, the girl's vagina is sewn shut, her legs are tightly tied together, and she is forced to lie on her side for several weeks until the two sides of her vagina heal together. And this is only the physical trial. While some people maintain that these women willingly and gratefully accept their fate, first-hand accounts collected from them largely debunk this notion. Published testimonies from Malian women speak of both physical and psychological trauma. Many grappled with the question of why their parents – those who were supposed to care for them and keep them safe – allowed them to be put through such a torturously painful procedure. In other cases, the women were subjected to it against the will of their female relatives, with the father or brother forcing them to get it done. What sort of imprint this must leave on their minds and hearts – and on the communal soul of all women – is beyond measure.

There's a law against female genital mutilation in Mali, but no-one pays much attention. Through these procedures, men are ensured a virgin at the time of marriage, when the woman's sealed vagina must be cut open for them. And if a jealous husband should happen to be going away for a period of time, he might insist that his wife be sewn back up again until he gets back. The resulting scar tissue and reduction of the vaginal opening means that both sexual intercourse and childbirth are exceedingly painful and difficult for her, yet this is the part no-one talks about. Instead, women are taught that their very femininity and fertility are at stake, and so that undesirable, unnecessary little appendage and its surrounding tissue must be removed at all costs.

The practice occurs among Malians of all religions. Among the more animist tribes like the Dogon, women are led to believe that they will remain in a sort of purgatory between man and woman until the 'little penis' is cut off. To them, having a clitoris is the antithesis of being a woman; the woman who still has hers remains hopelessly androgynous. Though the removal of the clitoris or external genitalia predates the introduction of Islam in West Africa, it has none the less been adopted most widely by Muslims, as a way to keep women chaste. Mali enjoys the classic double standard typical of misogynistic cultures – that a man may enjoy his sexual freedom, enjoy the sexual act itself, but a woman cannot. Malian men have told me that they consider the removal of a girl's clitoris a *favour*, a way to protect her from her own dangerous sexual urges. Better to obviate her sexual drives altogether, for her own good. After all, a woman's role is one of childbearing and motherhood, nothing more.

It's been hard for me to go to these villages when I know that most of the women I see have had their clitorises and

labia sliced off, their vaginas sewn shut with catgut. I have
trouble holding back my anger. Back in Old Ségou, the
Bambarra village where I first began my river trip, the girls
have the procedure done at the ripe age of sixteen. *Sixteen*.
By that time, presumably, the psychological trauma and
physical pain is enormous. And it's not just the ordeal of the
practice that I mourn; it's the ensuing medical compli-
cations that follow women for the rest of their lives.
Chronic bladder infections, difficult and painful urination
and menstruation, fibroids, sterility – even death.

Some Western apologists and post-colonial theorists still
euphemistically call this procedure 'female circumcision'
(as if it were a quaint initiation into womanhood and
nothing more, equivalent to the removal of a male's fore-
skin). Furthermore, I have heard such individuals lambasting
Western concern or involvement, claiming that any
Westerner who cares about the welfare of women in Africa
can only be operating from a manipulative or patronizing
colonialist stance. This is patently absurd. Basic humanistic
interests and concern for women's health seem reason
enough for Westerners *and* non-Westerners – men and
women alike – to care and become involved in defeating
this practice. Assitan Diallo, one of Mali's foremost advo-
cates for the banning of female genital mutilation, explains
what role she believes Westerners should have in this issue:
'We should keep in mind that many Westerners have more
experience in dealing with the subject than we do, because
they were the first to talk about it. And now we are also
talking about it . . . But I don't think I can be in the same

group with them to fight something in my own country, because I will feel, "Here they go again, colonization" ... So in my view, they can be like advisers.'

I paddle past the occasional village, waving back at the women doing their washing in the river, comforted by their cheers for me, their interest in my journey as a lone woman. I answer the men's questions, tell them where I'm going and enjoy the stunned looks on their faces when they hear 'Timbuktu'. In virtually all ways, I'm completely defying the traditional paradigm of a Malian woman: I don't have a man accompanying me; I do the paddling myself; I am self-sufficient and answer to no-one.

I decide to spend the night in a village, and I paddle to the only one I can see on a barren stretch of river. It's a collection of a few round adobe huts, topped with thatch. Some women, large washtubs balanced on their heads, see me as I paddle over, and they run off to alert the village. Pretty soon, everyone who can walk, run or crawl is awaiting me on shore.

I learn that this village is called Seerangoro. The women all wear large gold discs in their earlobes, the older women having several piercings up and down each ear. They style their hair in beautiful, elaborate cornrows with tufts of hair sticking up on top. Their skin is lighter-coloured, a dark blue tattoo accentuating the area around the mouth. They bare their breasts with wonderful nonchalance, brightly patterned *pagnes* covering the areas that Malians consider sexual: the legs and buttocks. They tell me they're Fulani – herders – and I can see their cows grazing near by, baying for the coming dusk.

Some African scholars believe that the Fulani migrated here many hundreds of years ago from the area near the Red Sea, bringing their herding ways to the Niger and other parts of West Africa. Their lives are inseparable from their cattle, which provide, in addition to milk and meat, a pastoral livelihood that enables them to survive without having to depend on fishing – unlike the Bozo or Somono. It is an independence that makes them wealthy, compared to many rural Malians. A single one of their cows, worth anywhere from $320 to $400, can sustain an entire family for more than a year.

The Fulani are also separated from their Malian compatriots by their appearance. Their light skin suggests Arab origins, and thus they associate themselves with the North Africans who brought writing and scholarship to West Africa, as well as organized religion. The Fulani are considered Mali's most pious tribal group, Islam playing a large role in their lives. It is a distinction in which they take pride, but is often a source of contempt from other indigenous peoples.

The Fulani children stroke my kayak and stare at me. No-one speaks a word of French, so I use some of the Bambarra I've learned. I ask them if they can bring me to the *doogootigi*, knowing from my experience in Sansanding that village etiquette along the Niger hasn't changed much over the centuries: you must always find the *doogootigi*, give him a gift for visiting his village, and ask him if he'll let you spend the night. Following this procedure is crucial, as it secures his hospitality and patronage, and thus ensures your safety.

I'm led to the chief. He's an old, hunched man who wears a grand smile. We shake hands. I pay him generously, and through a smattering of Bambarra and signs ask if I can spend the night. He quickly says yes, and instructs the kids to help bring my bags up to the village. They fight with each other to have the privilege of carrying up the kayak itself, the red boat held aloft by scores of little hands. As it only weighs twenty-three pounds, they easily hold it above their heads, cheering as if in a victory celebration, and place it beside the chief's hut. The same thing had happened at Sansanding – I returned from my walk around town to find my kayak safely deposited in Yaya's living room. I find it strange that none of the village people is comfortable leaving my kayak tied in the Niger beside their canoes, but must carry it to the village for safe keeping. Not that anyone would steal or damage it; rather, I think they consider it such a strange and valuable object that it must be kept close at hand.

The women crowd around me, holding up a single finger and speaking in fervent Bambarra. I'm unsure what the finger means, until one woman says two words in their language that I recognize: 'husband' and 'where'. I gesture to them that I'm alone. This they cannot believe. They point to the river, then to me, holding up a finger again and pretending to paddle.

I nod. Yes. Alone.

One woman named Ba claps her hands and grins. 'Alone,' she says, like a sigh. She turns to her friends and repeats the word.

The chief's wife comes over with an enormous gourd bowl, full of foaming cow's milk, straight from the udder. Growing up in a Chicago suburb, this is the closest I've ever come to country living. I tentatively sniff the milk. It even *smells* like a cow, which for some reason surprises me, but I lift the bowl and start to drink, and discover it to be delicious.

I take out of the kayak some uncooked rice I bought in Ségou and some fresh fish I bought from a Bozo fisherman, showing them to the women, telling them I'd like to offer them to the village for dinner. They assume I know how to prepare and cook these things because I'm a woman, so they bring out a cooking pot and various implements. I amuse them with my ineptitude. I stare at the rice, the women waiting for me to do something with it. When I put some in the cooking pot, they look at each other, suppressing laughs: I must *clean* the rice first – don't I know this? One woman takes over, showing me how to inspect the rice for impurities before washing it several times in a bowl. Finished, she hands it back to me. Now I put the rice in the cooking pot, but the women are laughing again: I must get the water to a *boil* first. They're patient with me, fascinated by my inability to accomplish even the most basic of domestic tasks. And how to explain that I don't know how to cook very well, that I've spent my life in the States, living on ramen noodles and macaroni and cheese? I'd make a lousy wife out here.

I look with apprehension at the fish. I know I must somehow gut them and remove the scales, but I've never done this before. My family never took me fishing; having never fished themselves. I buy my fish pre-cut in little Styrofoam containers in the Wal-Mart meat department. I take out my Swiss Army knife and start puncturing one of the fish bellies. The women are laughing uproariously now: I must take the scales off first. So I try to do so with the knife, but make such a mess of it that again one of the women takes over. She uses a blunt stick to remove them quickly and gently, then guts each fish, throwing the innards to nearby dogs.

We stuff ourselves on rice, listening to West African music on a transistor radio. Little kids dance to the beat, shuffling their bodies and sidestepping. They love music and dance here, each person trying to better the other's moves. In the midst of it, the grandparents spread out on mats with blankets over their heads, snoring loudly. One woman brings out a treasured page she's kept from a French magazine, which shows an advertisement of a white woman reclining on a luxurious bed with pink satin sheets. They point to the photo and then to me, as if that woman and I were somehow related.

Do they think I recline on pink satin sheets back home, in a flowing gown of silk, living a life of such luxury and ease? Do they see all white women in such a way: the Peace Corps person who comes by once a year, the anthropologist, the aid worker? I have no language in common with them, no means of explaining otherwise. I am trapped in the image they have of me, in that room with the satin sheets.

The women want to know many things from me. First of all, where is my husband, and why did he let me paddle on the Niger all by myself? They also want to know how many babies I have back home in America. I try my best to explain through signs and broken Bambarra why none of these things apply, but it takes some time, so that we're still discussing it long after dinner. I'm afraid we might be discussing it all night, but the women at last grow satisfied and declare it's bedtime.

We all lie down side by side on foam mattresses spread outside the huts. Mosquito nets stretch overhead, blurring the stars. Fleas hop on my skin; chickens jump on us. I fall asleep to the sound of the old folks' snoring, goats nibbling at our feet.

Always, in the midst of these kinds of trips, I reach a point when I suddenly wake up to the reality of what I'm doing. I discover, quite unexpectedly, that I am alone in a little red boat, paddling a river in the South Sahara *en route* to Timbuktu. This becomes news to me, as if it had all been unreal until now, and I'm forced to pull over to ponder the implications for the first time. Inevitably, I pull out my map. It tells me that I'm now past the town of Massina, and that my goal of Timbuktu rests so far to the north-east that it actually hides on another section of the map.

*My God*, I think, but always when it's too late. Always

when, as is the case now, a crowd of at least fifty children are running over a nearby hill and descending upon my boat.

'*Tubabu! Donnez-moi cadeau!*' they scream. 'Hey, whitey! Give me a gift!'

Their excitement turns chaotic. Hands are everywhere, pulling and grabbing at the things in my kayak. I take out a bag of dried pineapple slices and throw them in the air, and the mass of bodies shoots towards the treats, kids fighting and tearing at each other. I have never seen anything like it, though I tend to think I've seen it all, and I paddle away as if for my life.

I wonder when Mungo Park's moment of realization struck. When he was captured by the Moors and a woman threw urine in his face? When he was so destitute that he was forced to sell locks of his hair for good-luck charms? Or perhaps it hadn't come until the second and last journey, when he left on his river trip in a rotting boat, in the company of his four remaining soldiers, one of whom had gone insane? 'Though all the Europeans who are with me should die, and though I were myself half-dead,' Park wrote in his final letter, 'I would still persevere; and if I could not succeed in the object of my journey, I would at least die on the Niger.' *Why didn't he turn back?* the reader must wonder. *What was wrong with the man?*

But I am starting to learn more about Park than ever before. I'm starting to understand. Once the journey starts, there's no turning back. That's just the way it is. The journey binds you; it kidnaps and drugs you. It deceives you with images of the end, reached at long last. You picture yourself arriving on that fabled shore. You see everything you promised for yourself. For Park, it might have been streets of gold, cool oasis pools, maidens cooing in his ear. For me, it is much simpler: French fries and air-conditioning.

I paddle around a bend and see a village up ahead that's crowded with people. It's market day there, and large canoes line up along the shore, one after the next, so that there's barely a free space. Market day is a weekly occurrence in nearly every Malian village of any size, and it falls on a different day of the week depending on where you are. This is the first market I've actually witnessed, and so I decide to paddle over to it to see it for myself.

This decision is not without a heady dose of fear. This part of Mali never sees white people, and certainly not a white woman in a kayak. I'm already anticipating the great commotion my arrival will cause. And it's strange, too, to be paddling across the river as if from nowhere, no tour guide accompanying me to explain my appearance, no-one to translate. Just me. Going peacefully to the market to try to buy some mangoes, as if there were nothing out of the ordinary about it.

The people don't notice me until I'm nearly at the shore, their attention fixed on the market proceedings. One young boy spots me now and lets out a wail so loud that it could startle a deaf person.

'*Tubab! Tubaaaab!*' he screams. White person! White person!

And the cry becomes part of a universal exclamation.

*White person!* My reception is not to be believed. Hundreds of people rush to the shore, to the very edge of the ten-foot-high clay embankment that borders the river. They all stare directly at me – this crowd easily dwarfs the huge reception I had at Sansanding. Children are so keen on having a look at me that they scramble down the bank, clinging to tree roots to get a good view. Women smile at me in sheer amazement. The volume of the crowd nearly knocks me from my boat.

'*Tu-baaab! Tu-baaab! Tu-baaaaab!*'

I sense no hostility here whatsoever, just unabashed curiosity. I smile at everyone, greet them in Bambarra with an excited '*Iniché!*'

The minute I speak, the crowd falls silent. Everyone looks at each other, stares back at me, and suddenly they laugh uproariously. It's too much: a lone white woman appearing out of nowhere, speaking their language. They can't seem to fathom it. No-one, I notice, speaks a shred of French. But for the smattering of Bambarra words I've learned, I would be unable to communicate with them at all.

I ask what village this is, and either my Bambarra is faulty or their amazement prevents them from understanding, but they look at me in rapt incomprehension and say nothing. I try again. And again, until at last a young boy makes sense of my gestures and announces that I've reached the village of Tuara.

I ask what people live here and get a mixed reply: 'Malaka', 'Fulani', 'Bozo', 'Bambarra' – even 'Tuareg'. I try to be matter-of-fact about my visit, nonchalantly stepping out of my kayak and tying it between some canoes. I hoist my little daypack to my back and stare up at the assemblage of people. The women are dazzling in their colourful sarongs and head-wrappings, the more wealthy among them sporting earrings and head decorations made of pure gold. Some wear their hair in a single braid down either side of their heads, gold rings woven into the locks. Some of them have their mouth areas tattooed dark blue and wear thick gold bands through the septa of their noses. They are a stunning, vibrant people.

Usually when I arrive in the midst of such crowds there will be someone who is especially calm and eager to come to my assistance. In this case, it is a woman with a radiant smile and a scarf of blue silk wrapped about her head. She smiles benevolently at me and encourages me to come up the embankment. I look back at my kayak with all my things inside, worried that something might be taken during my absence, but she merely smiles at me as if she knows what my concerns are. She shakes her head as if to say, *Don't worry* and, trusting her implicitly, I start to climb the mud bank. When I slip, the entire crowd acknowledges it in a single loud grunt of concern. Hands reach out to help me up, and soon everyone presses close to me to touch my skin and hair, to stare at my face, my blue eyes. I stare back at the faces, just as amazed to be so close to them. I stare at the dark blue tattoos of the Malaka people, the bright gold nose bands, the smooth brown skin and welcoming eyes.

I can barely move without stepping on someone's foot, so my benefactor with the blue headscarf says a few magic words to the crowd that cause them to move back from me. I head towards the market to see what there is to be seen. Some Tuareg men – a North African Berber people, far from their traditional lands further north in Mali – leave their stalls to get a better look at me. They're the first Tuareg I've seen in person, are completely cloaked in dark purple indigo wrappings save for hazel eyes that peer out at me. They carry swords strapped to their waists, and stand proudly with their arms crossed, inspecting me.

The market is full of various services and wares: shoe repair, kola nuts, dates, seed pods of various sorts, cooking pots, silverware. I see mangoes for sale and head over, a large group of people following in my wake. The mangoes cost a trifle – seven cents apiece. I can tell from the price that the stallholders here never see white people, let alone tourists; the going tourist price for a mango in Ségou was sixty cents. I buy several of the fruit, telling the woman to keep the change, and as I deposit them inside my backpack, children take turns petting my arms and stroking my hair. Other children, though, are scared to approach, and I think of something Park wrote: 'A few women and children expressed great uneasiness at being so near a man of such an uncommon appearance.' Indeed, I must look like some apparition to the youngest kids, many of whom may never have seen a white person before.

I pass through the market for a while, admiring the clay pots that the local women make, enjoying such unusual company all around me. I never know what perception a particular village will have about me, but when they accept me, as this one has (and as the Fulani did the previous night), the experience is pure delight. I forget my usual fears of paddling through an unfamiliar country, alone. All I can think about is how extraordinary this world and its people are.

I return to my kayak. It's where I left it, its contents unmolested, though it has been retied closer to shore for better protection between two large canoes. Children, half submerged in the river, finger the kayak's rubber skin. They look up at me, grinning nervously as I approach as if I've caught them being naughty. I just smile at them. My benefactor with the silken scarf shakes my hand as I bid her goodbye.

'Where are you going?' she asks in Bambarra.

'To Timbuktu,' I say.

'To Timbuktu?! Eh!' She turns to the crowd and announces this information in a shout, and the whole crowd cheers. Just one big blast of voices.

Everyone lines up along the bank to watch me leave – such colourful, gracious people. I untie my kayak and get in, yelling thank you and goodbye in Bambarra. The crowd responds with arms held aloft, hands waving. Just hundreds of people, waving and cheering me on. I paddle off, and it's a while before the last boy stops running after me along the bank, bidding me a fervent farewell.

\*

I've been paddling for days now, staying at villages, and at last some familiarity greets me: Rémi, the magazine photographer covering my trip. He waits in a large *pinasse*, or river barge, that's docked by the town of Diafarabé. He waves and calls me over, aiming at my face an enormous telephoto lens that looks like a bazooka. I feel the old self-consciousness emerging. I've got used to being alone. Just me and the world, meeting anew at every turn. And now it's as if the glorious reunion has ended. I'm being pulled back to some reality I thought I'd left behind in a previous life – a reality of magazine issues and photography concerns. To me, it's like a sudden invasion of privacy. Still, I know I'll barely see him on this trip. He has orders to follow me upstream, take some pictures, and then promptly disappear again for days. It's the best compromise I could hope for.

I straighten my hat and smooth back my hair. I think of all the sunscreen smeared on my face, and of the sun-scorched redness of my cheeks. Self-consciousness is a strange, insidious disease. I would have thought I'd have abandoned it by now, make-up free as I am, mud-smeared, greasy-haired, flea-bitten. But here it comes, with a power of its own, telling me that I'm not prepared for having the image of my face transferred on to countless rolls of film that thousands of people may view some day. I quickly put on my sunglasses.

Rémi continues to wave me closer to his boat – closer to that monster camera lens he holds. He adopts an obliging, almost obsequious demeanour that must work well for

93

coaxing reluctant people like me into his photographs. Gifted and gregarious, and an excellent photographer, he's shot for many reputable publications in the West and finds himself 'in demand' in the business, magazines soliciting him for his work. It had been hard to find someone willing to paddle for weeks with me in the Saharan sun who also happened to be an expert photographer (the National Geographic folk are especially picky about their photography). Not to mention that photographers' rates tend to be quite expensive – anywhere from $400 to $600 a day (writers, on the other hand, are paid only for the finished article, regardless of how many days they spend in the field). And so they solicited Rémi. He offered his services to the magazine at a bargain price, but with the concession that he be allowed to bring his girlfriend along (as his 'assistant', he explained – a fairly common practice in his business), rent a large, motorized river barge and hire three Malian men to do such things as cook meals, handle the boat and set up the couple's tent each night.

Rémi's camera finds me now, the telephoto lens clicking away as I paddle alongside his boat. I feel like some sort of B-grade movie star with Rémi as my paparazzi. Half the town of Diafarabé has gathered to see what the big deal is, and they strain their eyes as if looking for something to justify all the hullabaloo. *Just me*, I want to tell them. My face and shirt covered with sweat, my bush hat crammed on my head, my arms crispy red. I suspect they're disappointed – hell, I would be. But it is enough of a show to see a lone white woman in an inflatable kayak.

There is the usual screaming and excitement from the kids – but perhaps more so this time, with all the picture-taking. I dip my hat into the water and put it back on to cool my head. It's hot – 97 degrees, according to my thermometer – and technically I've barely entered the South Sahara. I know the heat will become worse, though it already feels as bad as I'd like it to get.

Rémi's girlfriend comes over to greet me. She's a lithe, pretty redhead from the States named Heather, a graduate of the Yale Theater School now living in Paris with Rémi. This is the first time, she tells me, that she's been to a place like this. A place as poor as Mali.

Yes. Poor. Mali is a place where people resell syringes and water bottles, fashion flip-flops from used car tyres. I've been to other countries just as poor, places like Madagascar and Bangladesh and Nepal, so that when I see Mali all around me, a strange numbness of familiarity comes over me. A numbness that is part acceptance, but part resignation too. Inevitably, I become filled with this strong desire to Do Something about it, which often succumbs to feelings of futility.

I look out at Diafarabé now, a collection of tightly winding streets and adobe dwellings constructed on a round peninsula that juts into the river. It looks reasonably prosperous to me, but I haven't got out of the boat to walk the streets.

I remember arriving in the Malian capital of Bamako on my first day. The poverty seemed to smack of truth to me: the red mud streets, the women without hands, begging for money. Donkey carts heaped with hay or rice or cooking pots, struggling to market. The very richest men cutting through it all in their slick black Mercedes, windows tinted to protect their eyes from more than just the sun. All of this, West Africa. Mali. Fourth poorest country in the world. A country that limps if it moves forward at all. The average income, $250 per family per year. If they're lucky. Or you could find yourself sleeping on the street corner in your mother's lap, like the children I saw, noses running, bellies distended. I kept passing out Malian money to the hands that reached towards me. Bills worth fifty cents, a dollar. I'd go back to the bank, get stacks of the small, crumbling confetti bills, try to pass them out to every needy person I met. I placed bills between the arm stumps of women with leprosy, and they asked me to place them in their little plastic pails instead so the local boys wouldn't rob them. Boys with the audacity to rob starving women without hands. The women apologized for the request, for inconveniencing me.

I'd stood before my dumpy hotel, looking down a street of hard-packed red clay turning slowly to mud in the drizzling rain. The air smelled alternately of rotting fruit and urine and diesel exhaust, ancient wrecks of cars groaning by, propelled by some mysterious force of human ingenuity. Women wore colourful *pagnes*, or sarongs, and sat on the sides of the street, selling mangoes or bananas laid out on tarpaulins. More prosperous vendors built themselves tiny wooden shacks, from which they sold cigarettes or writing materials or the ubiquitous Coca-Cola (always drunk on-site, the returned bottles worth more than the soda inside).

I walked for miles down dirt streets lined with great shade trees, bordered by gutters full of raw sewage. I passed old women with leprosy, missing hands and feet, begging in the dirt. There were blind women. Women suffering from AIDS with small children in their arms. Boys with legs contorted behind them by polio, rolling around the street on crude trolleys. The poverty greeted me on every street corner and along every road. I quickly ran out of spare change or bills to drop in all the extended palms.

Interested in African art, I asked passers-by for directions to the National Museum. Their directions led me to the edge of town, to a fenced-in area: a field of rubble.

'Is this the National Museum?' I asked a passing man.

He nodded.

'Here?'

He nodded.

I surveyed the rubble. For some reason, none of the people giving me directions mentioned that there was no actual museum to speak of. It was indicative of a country still struggling to find its footing amid the idealism and corruption of post-independence days. We needed to be content that there was a place for a museum, and rubble to represent it, for these were signs of hope. Day and night, Bamako's heat was thick and tropical, like an uncomfortable blanket wrapped around me. I returned to town.

I wandered through the *grand marché*, or central market, which extended well beyond the main cement building into a chaotic labyrinth overtaking street after street. Nearly anything could be found there, if one had the endurance to travel down the unending lanes of wares. Dealers usually specialized in a single product: ballpoint pens, safety pins, plastic bags made from fertilizer sacks, used American T-shirts printed with basketball team logos or rock stars' visages. One area, devoted exclusively to butchered meat, displayed animal parts in various stages of preparation; I watched where I walked to avoid stepping in the blood puddles. Thrifty consumers crowded around fly-covered sheep heads and cow tongues and tails – the cheapest meats – while piles of shiny offal rested like plum-coloured pudding in plastic basins at the merchants' feet. It was nearing 90 degrees and there was no refrigeration, but this didn't seem to bother any of the people making purchases. Black clouds of flies landed and flew from one piece of meat to another. Cowed dogs crept beneath tarps, stealing away scraps.

I stopped at a vendor selling bolts of colourfully printed cotton cloth, commonly used for women's *pagnes* and tops, and bought a couple of metres. Going next door, to where men and women sat behind foot-operated sewing machines making people's clothes, I paid an old man to make me a couple of skirts for my kayaking trip. You could order anything there, and it would be made in a matter of minutes by expert hands. I explained that I'd like elastic at the top – a preference of practicality over the wrapped sarong – and he gave a boy some money and sent him off. The boy returned out of breath, handing over rolls of elastic. My waist and leg lengths were quickly measured, the man sat down to his machine, and ten minutes later he handed over two skirts, hemmed and pleated. When I asked how much, he stated his price in Malian money: $1.50. He looked at me warily; I could tell he thought he had overcharged me. When I doubled the amount and handed it to him, he touched it to his forehead and smiled a toothless grin.

I decided to visit the fetish market, a taboo and sacred place on the outskirts of the main market. While most cities or towns have one, foreigners are not encouraged to visit, and people are forbidden to take photos. The two drivers I flagged down refused to drive me there. Many Malians believe these markets are places of dark magic, and not for casual viewing by foreigners or interlopers.

People go to them in order to purchase ingredients for different spells, animist traditions remaining such an integral part of West African culture that they're still practised by many members of the Christian or Islamic faiths. Most Malians carry *grigri* charms full of special ingredients or prayers meant to protect them from life's myriad unfavourable circumstances. There are ways to alter nearly everything that happens – well-established spells and rituals that can effect some control over future or external events. Sick children can be saved, infertile women brought to child, businessmen blessed with riches. But the correct products must be purchased, the proper rituals performed. Witch doctors were generally consulted for such purposes, employing a number of magical methods to achieve the desired result. The more difficult and demanding the request, the greater and more expensive the ingredients or sacrifices needed for the spell. Thus clients receive a laundry list of necessary items and go shopping at the fetish market.

I spent an hour searching for the place until a friendly Indian store owner told me exactly where it was. Located on the far edge of the market, it took up a wide swath and was full of vendors with tarps laid on the ground on which were myriad dried-plant concoctions and animal body parts. The air smelled putrid. Men held up rotting monkey heads, dried lizards, snakeskins, waving them in my face as I walked by. Every conceivable item was represented there, from leopard paws to antelope testicles. Many of these animals couldn't be found in Mali – or even in West Africa – and had to have been imported over vast distances.

A fetish dealer called me over. He whispered something and opened a metal box. Flies rushed out into the sunlight, and I saw a live cayman and a falcon inside. The cayman was completely bound up with cord, its slat eyes levelled on mine. The bird, mouth open in thirst, shook from fear, its mahogany-coloured feathers rumpled and filthy, its legs and wings tied tightly with string. I imagined buying it, setting it free. But it would be replaced by a new one. A cycle. The endless, nearly untouchable suffering . . .

Heather asks me how my trip's been so far.

'Fine,' I say, which is what I say when I don't feel like explaining how I really feel about anything. For example, how I'm embarrassed about being photographed by Rémi right now. How when I was staying in Prague I used to always walk several blocks out of my way to avoid being photographed by all the tourists on the Charles bridge.

'It's pretty damn hot,' I say to her.

'Yeah, it is!' Her pale skin is flushed, and beads with perspiration. Rémi tells me he's been waiting for me all morning in this heat. And as the afternoons don't provide any decent lighting, there's been nothing for him to take pictures of. Just the waiting. He says he's been reading a good book about the explorations of René Caillié.

Heather rests under the pirogue's awning, drinking bottled water and trying to escape from the sun. I look down the Niger, in the direction I have to go. The shores on either side appear dusty and parched, holding few trees. Such a long way to Timbuktu. I feel that slice of panic and horror in my gut: why this crazy journey? I wonder what Rémi and Heather think about my trip, the idea of kayaking some six hundred miles on this river, in this heat, for no reason that could ever sound logical. I'm reminded of the men of history who claimed to have climbed a mountain 'because it's there', but I don't believe them for a minute. We are all at the mercy of a whole slew of forces that are more easily ignored than faced. Forces out of childhood, forces from present causes and conditions, forces as enigmatic as life itself, that tell us we must try to achieve something or get somewhere. No expedition, no journey, no personal challenge seems a product of whim or accident, initiated because something is simply 'there'.

I wait until the camera stops clicking, wring out my long-sleeved shirt in the waters of the Niger, and put it on in an attempt to cool off. Time to go. I bid *kambe* – goodbye – to the watching crowd, wave goodbye to Rémi and Heather and their crew. Rémi gives me instructions to wait for him at a particularly picturesque village downriver called Koa.

# CHAPTER FIVE

I APPROACH KOA AFTER TEN HOURS OF PADDLING, having passed villages where everyone lined up on shore, beating on drums and yelling at me for no apparent reason. It is the first time I've experienced such hostility on my trip, and I can't account for it. I pull out my map and see that, geographically, I'm near the inland city of Djenné, conquered or controlled by various peoples throughout history – Moors, Malians, Songhai, Moroccans, French – which might explain the region's unusual suspicion towards foreigners. Djenné itself is the site of the largest mud mosque in the world, and it once competed with Timbuktu as the scholarly headquarters for Islam in West Africa. Today, it remains a very sacred place, inhabited by people who are said to be the most pious and orthodox of Mali's Muslims. Even Mungo Park strictly avoided Djenné on his first brief journey on the Niger. He wrote, 'I was apprehensive that, in attempting to reach ... Jenné, I should sacrifice my life to no purpose.' He reported that the people of Djenné had different roots from Malians further south, speaking a different language, and concluded that the Moorish presence there made an attempted visit too dangerous.

I see from my map that today's journey probably took me past Park's turnaround point on that first trip. He stopped 'two short days' journey' from Djenné, which would place him near Koa. This means that I've officially reached Park's point of no return, and it gives me the creeps.

I recall the kindly villages I passed earlier on, full of children's waves of greeting, wondering if a mere change in geography can explain people's reactions to me. All I know is that, from now on, I'll be unable to draw any satisfying conclusions about any of the villages I pass. This is un-settling. Better they be one way or the other, better I'm able to forecast something – anything – about them during this trip. I keep looking for something substantial and permanent, something to count on, and yet I'm constantly unhinged by the sheer unpredictability of what I discover each day. I feel as if I'm paddling more and more into some kind of unknown, the heat rising each day, the sun more dazing. Mungo Park must have experienced the same thing, this world of West Africa confounding him with its lack of guarantees. And there is a certain point when you acquiesce to the discomfort of not knowing, and I'm almost there. I can feel the burn-out that inevitably precedes the giving in, the end of all resistance.

The torn muscle in my arm throbs, but the other muscles seem to have compensated for it and I find it doesn't hurt as much as before. This is a blessing I hadn't counted on, assuming it'd only get worse. I was actually thinking I might have to stop this trip if it did, if the pain became too excruciating, or if my arm completely gave out. But it's as if my arm knew I wasn't going to stop, for all its complaining, and so my body did what it could to handle the problem, strengthening other muscles in place of the weakened one, healing the injury at some mysterious level.

Rémi chose to meet me at Koa mainly because of the large mud mosque close to the river. It is a photographer's dream shot, the spiky minarets casting a raw, primal beauty on to the silver spread of the Niger. A stream cuts through town, adobe homes rising on either side and connected by an arcing bridge made of palm trunks and planks of wood. During the height of the rainy season, the stream floods and the two sides of Koa are cut off from each other completely. To stare at Koa is to enter pure imagination, the wondrous worlds of childhood fancy. It's a place that seems too far, too foreign to ever breathe life outside my mind. I watch the Niger unfurling waves against the low clay shore, men striding by in long silk *grand bubu* robes that reach to their knees, and the women, hair plaited with gold, bend over the river in *pagnes* and head-wrappings of such bright colours, such intensity, that my eyes suffer to take it all in.

The crowds on shore spot me as I paddle towards them, and finally something becomes familiar: the exclamations, the stares of people confounded by what they see, the rushing of women and children down to the river to get a better look. Men throw down the nets they're mending. Goats scream and run out of the way. Chickens dash for cover. It is utter mayhem, and I am the sole cause.

I smile at the people as I drag my kayak on to shore. They press in so close to me, however, that I'm unable to move any more, and so I stand in the midst of the groping hands and loud questions, helpless. An old man comes up behind the crowd with a large stick and, incredibly, starts striking people hard on their backs. The crowd disperses immediately, and I'm afforded a small passageway through which to walk.

'Where's the chief?' I ask in Bambarra and then in French. The old man points beneath an ancient tree, which I should know by now is the best place to find any chief in Mali. I walk up to the *doogootigi* and greet him. Another thing that's familiar to me by now: he frowns at me. I pull out some bills for a *cadeau* and put them in his hand, asking if I can spend the night. He takes my money, counts it, smells it, and pockets it casually like some kind of Godfather. His face releases no hint of a smile. The old man with the big stick steps forward, tells me his name is Seku Mayantawa, and that he'll put me up for the night. I agree.

I grab my backpack from the kayak, and with Seku walking before me, beating away onlookers, we reach his home. It's a collection of several adobe huts forming a large courtyard. He spreads out a mat under a veranda and instructs me to sit down. Several little kids run in with my kayak balanced on their heads, and they drop it beside me. Following them is a crowd even larger than that on the shore, and the people surround me, staring and exclaiming. Some of them in the front row sit down so that the people behind them can see better. They are not, I notice, going anywhere any time soon.

I sigh. I give some money to Seku as a gift, hoping he'll eventually run everyone out of here. One of his wives pushes through the crowd to enquire what I'd like for dinner. She offers chicken and noodles, which sound like delicacies to me. As payment, I give her a large silver coin I brought from home, and she presses it to her chest, thanking me. Another ally, I hope. More people crowd into the courtyard until there's nowhere to walk.

And now I experience another familiar, all-too-annoying problem that has become a trademark of this trip: being surrounded by an entourage of people when I have to pee. That's one thing the explorers of old never wrote about – how they managed to relieve themselves in these oddball places. The difficulties – not to mention dangers – that Sir Edmund Hillary must have experienced whipping it out on the top of Mount Everest. That sort of thing.

I sit down on my mat, looking at everyone, staring at them as they stare at me: the women's intricate cornrows, the boys' little mohawks. One boy holds a deflated football, and I convince him to hand it over to me. I take out my kayak's foot pump and blow up the ball, sealing the faulty valve with a piece of duct tape. The crowd is amazed by the pump, the tape, amazed by the bag of tricks that I have with me, and they're all barely a foot away from me now, gazing down at the football that I've just made functional. I toss the ball back to the boy, but it just bounces off his chest. He stares at me, paralysed with surprise.

'Ça va?' I ask him, smiling.

He just looks at me, another boy grabbing the ball and running away with it.

A man pushes through the crowd to greet me. From his proud deportment and fine white shirt, I can tell he's someone important in Koa. He shakes my hand and his fingers linger in mine longer than I'd prefer. I remove my hand from his and start taking notes.

'Are you a writer?' he asks in perfect French.

'Yes,' I say.

'Are you married?'

'I hope not.'

'I don't understand.' He leans close to me, smiling. 'Are you married?'

'Not to my knowledge.'

His eyes are levelled on mine. Too much intimacy in his stare. I ask Seku how many people live in Koa, hoping the other guy will go away.

'One thousand five hundred,' Seku says.

'What tribe is this?'

'Bozo.'

It's the first Bozo village I've stayed at, and already I'm not liking it much. I miss the Fulani villages with the cows wandering everywhere and the calabashes of warm milk, and the gentle hospitality that made me feel safe and at home. Here, with the close, gaping crowds, it feels like a madhouse. I'm experiencing exactly what Park must have two hundred years ago, while staying in another large Malian village.

I was so completely surrounded by the gazing multitude, that I did not attempt to dismount. [A messenger] had orders to procure me a lodging, and see that the crowd did not molest me. He conducted me into a court, at the door of which he stationed a man, with a stick in his hand, to keep off the mob, and then shewed me a large hut, in which I was to lodge. I had scarcely seated myself ... when the mob entered; it was found impossible to keep them out, and I was surrounded by as many as the hut could contain. When the first party, however, had seen me, and asked a few questions, they retired, to make room for another company; and in this manner the hut was filled and emptied thirteen different times.

The guy with the white shirt is still lingering. I get up to take a walk around town, hoping I won't be treated to my own thirteen visits by 'the mob'. If I'm lucky maybe I can find a private moment to relieve myself in the not-so-discreet mud hole behind Seku's house. I walk across the stream cutting through town, past a storefront with an Osama bin Laden picture hanging on the wall. A slice of fear cuts through me. The crowd, rather than leaving, simply follows behind me in a long stream of onlookers. It is absolutely impossible to be alone.

I return to the courtyard. Someone has spread out a foam mattress for me to sleep on, as it's too hot to sleep inside one of the buildings. I sit down on it to do some writing before Seku's wife finishes dinner, the crowd reassembling around me. I try to ignore everyone now, and people sit down near by, whispering. The more industrious among them ask in poor French, 'Donnez-moi cinq cent francs.' Give me five hundred francs. New groups of onlookers arrive to replace the few stragglers heading home for dinner. No-one does anything but watch me as if I were a particularly provocative zoo animal.

I manage to get some writing done. Night comes, and Seku brings a kerosene lamp for my use, bugs sailing against it and crashing into me. The crowd murmurs whenever I do something – pulling insect bodies from my hair, eating a chicken drumstick, turning a page of my journal. I remember visiting the zoo as a kid, and how I'd ooh and aah at the chimpanzees when they peeled a banana or picked a bug from their arm. In Koa, I'm just another hairy simian. Exhausted from all the paddling today and wanting to go to bed, I ponder ways of getting rid of the crowd that won't involve borrowing Seku's club – which seems to be the most effective form of Malian crowd dispersal to date. It's one thing to ignore everyone when I'm writing, but I know I'm not going to be able to sleep very long with nearly a hundred people gathered around me all night, listening to me snore.

I have an idea: I will set up my tent on the foam mattress. But, predictably, the tent construction only brings more people dashing into the courtyard to see the show. Fortunately, I have a small backpacking tent that sets up quickly. I make sure I put on the rain flysheet so no-one can look inside. Climbing in, I experience the first bout of privacy I've yet had in Koa. It's incredibly hot with the rain fly on and no air flow, the 98-degree heat from the day still thick in the air. I sit and take a sweat bath, waiting for the people outside to get bored and go home. My plan works. (Poor Mungo could have used a tent like mine to save him from this.) The crowd starts to disperse, but I keep peeping outside to make sure no-one is left. Finally: freedom. I creep out of the tent and run to Seku's mud hole to take my long-awaited bathroom break.

If you can sleep anywhere in a village along the Niger, the roof of an adobe house is the best place to do it. I take down my tent and sneak up clay steps to the top of Seku's house. Only Koa's mosque is higher than I am now. I spread my sleeping pad on the hard clay of the roof, the stars in a dazzling spread above me, a light breeze drying my sweat-covered clothes. I lie down and study the stars for a while, picking out Cassiopeia and Pegasus, watching the moon rising over the huts to the east. No-one to bother me. No-one knowing I'm here—

I hear footsteps. The man with the crisp white shirt and lingering handshake climbs up the stairwell and walks over to me.

'*Bonsoir, mademoiselle,*' he says, smiling.

'Yeah. *Bonsoir*,' I say.

'You aren't married, are you? I don't see a ring.'

'Nope,' I say in English. And in French: 'I want to sleep now.'

'Yes,' he says. 'Of course. Tell me, do you have a boyfriend?'

'In America,' I lie.

'But he is in America and you are here.'

A clever man. I prepare my bed, knowing where this conversation is headed. All I know is that I'm not in the mood.

'Do you want a Malian boyfriend?' he asks.

'I thought you'd never ask,' I say.

'Miss?'

'I don't want a boyfriend. I want to sleep now.' I look him in the eye; I make sure I can get up quickly, in case I have to defend myself.

'Give me your address. I will write to you.'

'Tomorrow,' I say. 'I want to sleep now.'

'Can I sleep here with you?'

I stand and point to the stairs. 'Go,' I say. 'Leave.'

'Why can't I sleep with you?'

'I'm going to hurt you,' I say in English. I look over the side of the roof and see the wife I'd given the silver coin to. I call to her.

'*Ça va?*' she yells up.

But the man is already heading down the stairs like a guilty child. Down below, I watch him stride across the courtyard, his white shirt glowing in the darkness. She follows him with her eyes then looks back at me.

'*Ça va, maintenant*,' I say. Everything's fine now.

'Don't worry,' she says. She closes the door of the court-yard behind him and locks it.

I lie down. The same stars greet me, but it's harder to see them. My heart beats louder in my chest.

Rémi arrives in the late morning. I can hear his boat long before I see it, the great engine chugging him down this long sweep of the Niger. It's not often that the people of Koa get visitors in one of the large river barges, so most of the town's population heads to shore to see who's coming. Me, I hide on the roof for as long as possible, to avoid the crowds.

When Rémi starts to get close to the village, I pack my things and leave my sanctuary. I walk to the river, the crowd promptly surrounding me. Kneeling down on the muddy bank, I wait, people pointing and gesticulating above me, pressing in from all sides. I'm not sure what his photo op is going to entail, and I'm ready to just leave Koa behind. I'm cranky today; I didn't sleep well last night. I kept waking, expecting the man in the white shirt to come up those stairs again to bother me. And what do Malian women do, if such a thing happens? Do they yell and kick him in the balls? Fortunately, I don't see him anywhere this morning. And anyway, Rémi's coming. Worst-case scenario, I can say the Frenchman's my boyfriend – a very jealous boyfriend with a bad temper.

I sigh and wait, and soon the large boat glides towards shore. I stand up to wave, in case Rémi can't see me in the mass of people. He's leaning off the side of the boat, camera in hand, another around his neck. The kids start up a heated chorus of '*Ça va! Ça va! Ça va!*'

'*Oui, oui*. OK. *Ça va, mes enfants, ça va, ça va.*' Rémi tries to quiet them, which proves impossible. '*Bonjour, Kira,*' he says to me instead. We eye each other knowingly: a mutual understanding of what it's like to be engulfed by these crowds, to be watched by hundreds of eyes, to lose all semblance of privacy.

Rémi gets out of the boat, followed by Heather.

I walk up to her. 'This place is a madhouse,' I warn her.

As if on cue, Seku, my benefactor, comes striding towards shore, wearing a straw hat and holding his stick. He starts whipping any bodies that cross his path. Kids screech and run off; young men give him a wide berth. Before long he's cleared a path for us.

Rémi says he'd like to get some shots around town, pictures of me looking at things and taking down notes. Kira-the-Writer type shots. So I follow him dutifully, and he has me sit on the end of the tall palm-trunk bridge with my pen and notebook. I try to look contemplative, staring off at the mosque, down at the river, at my notes. I've never done this sort of thing before, and I feel utterly ridiculous.

We head into the narrow streets for more photos. Seku follows, wielding his switch at the kids who wander into Rémi's shots. I sit at the end of long alleyways, pretending to write in my notebook, while Rémi shoots from different angles and with different lenses. I stand beside Seku in particularly photogenic locations and hold mock conversations with him while the cameras go off. An hour passes in this way. Rémi's supply of film seems endless.

Seku takes us into the big mosque for some canned shots on the roof. It's a rare privilege for a white person, a non-Muslim, to be allowed to enter a mosque in Mali, but Seku is a good guy for all his ardent switching of the kids. The mosque is bare inside but for a podium. I was expecting something akin to the ostentation of a Buddhist temple or a Christian church, but there are no paintings or gilded figures or elaborate filigree altars inside; nothing but white walls. I sit in the dim emptiness against a pillar, in a shaft of sunlight, trying to look profound for Rémi's photos. Heather, being thoughtful, runs forward to hide my bra strap. Rémi alternates between giving me rapid directions and praising the way I'm standing or holding my head, as if I were in the middle of a *Vogue* shoot. Seku stands off to one side, watching it all, uncomprehending.

It couldn't be easy being a photographer and doing this sort of thing. I give Rémi a lot of credit. Just the idea of arriving suddenly and sweeping through town with cameras in hand, before anyone realizes what's happening. Having to deal with writers like me, who find it all bizarrely absurd. Having to clear the kids away from shots, and placate village officials, and make sure you have enough spare change to pay off all the locals. Rémi has a certain deferential quality to his demeanour and speech, uses an interesting combination of flattery and forcefulness that gets him the shots he's known for in the magazine business; people – including me – tend to acquiesce readily to his wishes. For him to do it any other way, to be too demanding or too accommodating, would surely be detrimental to his work.

We head up to the roof of the mosque, the spiky mud minarets surrounding us like castle turrets. The Niger passes in the distance to my right; to my left, beyond the border of the town, I see only cultivated green fields. Rémi has me sit down next to Seku and hold another pretend conversation with him.

'That's right, Kira, look at him. Turn your head. Now look at me. That's great. That's perfect. Now look at him again. Talk to him.' And on it goes. I look at Seku, at his old, wrinkled face.

'I'm sorry about this,' I whisper to him in French.

He tells me it's all right; he is my comrade-in-the-absurd. And finally Rémi is done, has acquired all the shots he thinks he needs in Koa, and he thanks me for being a good sport. Now he'll take photos of my departure on the Niger, and then I'll be on my own again.

I head back to the shore, some little kids with mohawks carrying my kayak back from Seku's house. I put my gear inside and get in, and Rémi has me paddle back and forth along the shore, pretending to be departing each time. I wave goodbye to the people over and over, and they play along, waving back, and at last the goodbye is for real. I find Seku in the crowd and give him a parting wave, and now it is the great Niger River again, and nothing to do but paddle. Rémi gives me the name of a hotel in Mopti, saying he'll find me there. His great boat chugs past to the north-east. I have the river all to myself again.

# CHAPTER SIX

I PADDLE DOWN A LONELY STRETCH OF THE NIGER, passing the occasional small village of thatch or adobe huts resting in heat waves. I travel in the middle of the river, hoping to preserve my distance from people on shore so that I won't create a ruckus. Sometimes I find it amazing that I'm doing this kind of trip, because I'm not what some would call an 'extrovert'. I've always valued solitude and anonymity, yet here I do nothing but attract attention to myself at every turn. For me, it's a bigger personal challenge approaching and propositioning people in villages for a place to sleep than actually doing all the paddling to Timbuktu. Before I left, friends back home asked me if I wouldn't be 'scared' travelling alone on this river, and I found it hard convincing them that I'd experience more anxiety arriving at strange villages. This trip pulls me out of my comfort zone like none other, out of a place that is usually so strongly fortified that I get reclusive.

On shore, several children shout when they see my kayak. They leave their village, running along the mud bank, yelling, beckoning. I wave to them, but I know better than to stop and risk being overrun by the crowd. Still, children are safe and artless. They always have curiosity, not ill intent. If I fear anyone, it is the adults. Men who might want to do me harm. I was warned, in particular, not to kayak alone in the vicinity of Mopti, because the city breeds malcontents, young men with boats of their own, looking to rob a 'rich *tubab*'. While I never forget my vulnerability on this river – it stays with me like an itch – I don't let it stop what I'm doing. I just tolerate it, adjust to it. Usually, it doesn't trouble me too much.

Until times like now.

There are four young men in a speedboat, fast approaching me. Boats with outboards are rarities on this river – this is only the second speedboat I've encountered since the beginning of my trip. Mali's utter poverty extends to its waterways, where the best most people can do is to rig sails to increase their speed. In a country with few roads, procuring enough petrol to run an outboard would preclude such a luxury for any but the wealthiest. This is all good news for me and my safety: in my swift, lightweight kayak, I can usually outrun even the most dogged pursuer in a dug-out canoe. But when faced with the speed and manoeuvrability of a speedboat, I have no way whatsoever to protect myself.

I can only hope that these men don't wish me any harm. I put my can of mace in my lap and paddle as quickly as I can towards shore. As the speedboat comes to a fast stop

KIRA SALAK

beside me, I continue paddling to try to prevent anyone onboard from grabbing hold of my kayak or the things inside. But too late – one man has seized my lead rope. He wraps it several times around his hand, pulling my kayak snug against the boat. Their outboard chugs and spits into the grey water.

'*Bonjour*,' the man says, standing over me. My mind runs over my options. They're few and abysmal. There's no escape in the middle of a river, nowhere to 'run' to. I can see a village about a half-mile ahead on the left-hand shore. If I have to, maybe I can convince these men to let go of my kayak so I can paddle to shore, get out, flee to the village.

'*Bonjour*,' I say impatiently from behind my sunglasses, not making eye contact, waiting for their inevitable request for *l'argent*, money. All I know is that it's important not to show fear. Better impatience or anger than fear. That lesson was grilled into me during my martial arts training – to not present myself as a lesser opponent, a victim. To feel and present an attitude of strength at all times.

'Give me money, *tubab*,' the man says in French. His friends extend their palms and make similar requests.

I do nothing.

'*Tubab*,' he says louder, as if I haven't heard him. '*Tubab*! Give me money.' He tugs on the lead rope wrapped around his hand.

I sit back, rest my elbows on the paddle, and wait. I have all the damn time in the world. I am prepared to sit here the entire afternoon if I have to. Luckily, my daypack with my money and passport is secured behind my seat today; if they

120

wanted to take it, they'd have to physically remove me from the kayak.

The man calls to me again, and when I don't respond for the third time, he and his buddies whisper among themselves in a tribal language.

'Do you speak French?' the man suddenly asks me in French.

I give him no answer. Reaching for my water bottle, I take a long sip and then chuck it between my feet.

'Money,' the man says in rough English. '*Psst, psst! Tubab!*'

The men start talking to each other again. I start to clean out the dirt from beneath my fingernails.

'Money,' the man says to me. He yanks at the lead rope, trying to get my attention. '*Tubab! Cadeau!*'

The children from the village I passed, who had been running along the shore all this time trying to keep up with my kayak, appear on the nearby bank. When they call out to me, I get a sudden idea: I vigorously beckon them with my hand. The crowd of boys exchange glances, and, hesitating for just a moment, dive eagerly into the river. Accomplished swimmers, they race each other to my kayak. When they reach me, out of breath, they grab hold of the side of my boat. They smile broadly at me as if in victory.

'*Ça va! Ça va!*' they yell to me.

'*Ça va!*' I yell in return.

My kayak isn't big enough to support all of them, so they start trying to climb into the speedboat. The men angrily order them out, but they've made it a game trying to get inside, and their little bodies start springing over the sides. The man in charge of the outboard revs it and starts to move the boat forward, but this doesn't deter the invaders. After more angry yells to them, he orders the release of my kayak and cranks the motor to full throttle. In an instant, the boat surges forward. Boys leap over the side, treading water as they watch the boat roar away down the river. Relieved, I pass out chunks of dried apricot to my saviours. We suck on the fruit together, smiling at each other, floating along with the Niger.

I never know how I'll handle these kinds of threatening situations until they arise. Yet, as a woman travelling alone, I know they're as inevitable as the changing weather along the Niger. The truth: my gender will always make me appear more vulnerable. But to not travel anywhere out of fear, or to remain immobilized in a state of hyper-vigilance when I do, feels akin to psychological bondage. I do not want to give away that kind of power.

The Niger churns and shifts in a strong wind. I paddle against the gales, barely creeping forward, hitting currents that propel me around bends and throw me into high waves. But there are no storms, at least. No rain. Just grey skies, and the unrelenting river that mocks all sense of progress. I pull over to a sandbar to rest and eat a Snickers.

I've developed a steady speed to my paddling that I can maintain for a couple of hours without stopping, my arm and upper-body muscles looking better-defined than they've ever been. After overcoming the psychological protests to beginning a day of paddling, my body settles into the routine of the up and down strokes. My stamina has greatly increased, as when I used to train every day as a runner, and for the first time during this trip, kayaking feels like a natural expression of my body, an extension of myself.

I've been hoping to reach Mopti today, and so of course the river and weather aren't co-operating with me. It seems more than mere coincidence that as soon as I want to get somewhere, all forces seem to marshal themselves towards preventing me. I think I can understand why the locals believe in a god of the river; why, when eating on the Niger, they drop a portion of their meal into the water as an offering. When you do the paddling yourself, when there's no outboard on your boat to do the work, when you must depend exclusively on the natural environment and your physical abilities to get anywhere, the Niger becomes more than a waterway – it becomes a personality. I understand implicitly what is meant by 'becoming one with nature' as soon as I'm obliged to rely on forces out of my control. And this is perhaps the strangest revelation about my journey to date, and the oddest transformation that I see occurring within me: I feel caught in a relationship with these waters. The paddling has become personal; the Niger has turned into a fickle parent making constant demands of me and thwarting all my plans.

Mopti represents my journey's halfway point, and my mind, hopelessly spoiled by First World luxuries, craves what I'll be able to find there. Hot showers, filling meals, flea-free beds. When I've asked fishermen how far away Mopti is, they never reply in terms of kilometres. Such a distance analysis is worthless when you're doing the paddling yourself and must face conditions that can't be predicted. Instead, invariably, they stare up at the sun and reply in terms of paddling hours. Ten hours, maybe. Or twelve hours, if there's a bad storm. Eight, possibly, but only with an agreeable river and fast paddling.

I get in my kayak again and paddle as fast as I ever have, but none of it is enough to get me anywhere near Mopti. The sun starts to set, and I circle bend after bend, straining my eyes for sight of a distant radio tower – the harbinger of all big towns along the river. The impatience and annoyance I'm feeling is reaching epic heights. But I see nothing, and I must just let go, resign myself to the fact that I won't reach Mopti or any of its comforts tonight.

I pass a single domed hut on the mud shore, constructed entirely from woven thatch mats. A man stands beside it and yells out to me in excellent French.

'Where are you going?' he asks.

'To Mopti,' I yell. And in my impatience, I again ask the familiar question: 'How far is it?'

He looks at the position of the setting sun. 'You'll get there at one in the morning,' he says with finality. It is the finality of a man who knows the river well, and I believe him. I see the futility of continuing.

'You're welcome to spend the night with me and my family,' he says. He's smiling and nodding graciously at me.

His little children join him, staring at me, fingers in their mouths. I take up his offer, paddling back against the current and pulling up on the mud bank next to his canoe.

His name is Blabasy Tapoo, and it turns out that he's a Somono man. The Somono are the Niger's great fishermen, rumoured to be the modern descendants of Nile River fishermen who emigrated across the Sahara in previous millennia. Mungo Park frequently wrote about the Somono – they were the ones he always entrusted with burying his dead. He also noted in his narrative the excellent fishing skills of a people who, given their techniques, were more than likely Somono: 'The fisherman paddled his canoe to the bank ... stripped off his clothes, and dived for such a length of time, that I thought he had actually drowned himself, and was surprised to see his wife behave with so much indifference upon the occasion; but my fears were over when he raised up his head astern of the canoe, and called for a rope ... At length, [he] brought up a large basket, about ten feet in diameter, containing two fine fish.' I see similar large baskets in Blabasy's canoe, each hand-made from strips of wood and cord. The traditions have barely changed over the centuries.

Blabasy ties up my kayak and takes me inside his little compound. He lives in an area of about twenty feet by twenty, surrounded by a thatch fence. Chickens roam about, pecking at scraps and racing from approaching children. A huge pile of firewood fills up nearly half the available space, with fishnets and underwater baskets lying on top. The straightforward simplicity of this life is obvious in the clay pots that hold millet and rice, the rolls of woven-thatch building material, the small oblong hut just big enough for the family to fit inside. Clay from the riverbank has been ingeniously moulded into a large oven for cooking. There is no sign of Western goods. No *need* for Western goods. All of the basics have been met. Everyone looks content and satisfied. If they need to relieve themselves, they walk off into the countryside. If they need to bathe, they have the Niger just a few feet away.

I give Blabasy a gift of some money, and he looks down at the bills with shy surprise: he wasn't expecting anything in return for his generosity. I meet Blabasy's two wives: an older woman named Niami and a girl who looks to be barely sixteen, whom at first I took to be Blabasy's daughter. But they marry young out here. Unlike the tattooed and decked-out Fulani women I've seen, these Somono women are unadorned but for small gold hoops in each ear. Both nurse babies; Blabasy tells me that he's the proud father of seven children, the two oldest with his sister in nearby Asawana village. He seems to be a good husband and dad, speaking kindly to his wives and bringing out a young daughter to bounce on his knee. I'm not surprised by the fact that he has more than one wife — it's the norm in Mali. According to Islamic law, each man is allowed a maximum of four wives, assuming he can provide for them; in the villages I've visited so far, two seems to be the going number.

As Blabasy is so unusually friendly and forthcoming, and as his great French enhances my ability to communicate with him, I want to ask him about having two wives. I'd rather ask the women themselves, but, as is the case throughout Mali, they are uneducated and have no knowledge of French whatsoever.

'Do you like having two wives?' I ask Blabasy. A stupid question, but I want to see what he says.

He speaks in a quick, stuttering, enthusiastic sort of way. He seems delighted and flattered to be answering my questions, and I'm a bit taken aback by his candour. 'When one wife is pregnant,' he says, 'I can sleep with the other.' He points to the younger woman. 'When neither is pregnant, I take turns. One night with her, one night with her.' He smiles grandly. 'I like it a lot.'

'Do they get jealous?' I ask.

'No, no. I'm good to them both.'

I'm wondering what the women think of the arrangement, but they do look happy together, sharing the cooking, chatting to each other. Blabasy orders the kids to catch a couple of chickens for our dinner, and his two young boys come back, each with a screeching bird in hand. Blabasy politely excuses himself to chop off the heads. He returns a minute later, passing the twitching bodies to the women. Picking up his little girl, he bounces her on a knee and baby-talks to her. He seems to have accepted the job of babysitting the kids while his wives cook.

'Do you want more wives?' I ask him.

He grins. 'Yes. But I must wait until I catch more fish during the rainy season, when I'll be rich again.'

He explains to me that he lives in this lone hut on the

riverbank because it's more convenient for his fishing. By setting up temporary camp here, instead of in Asawana, which is inland, he can more easily catch and sell his fish. But it's the slow season now, as the rains have only just started, and the big fish harvests won't come until a few months from now. 'In December I'll be a rich man,' he says.

'What will you do until then?' I ask.

'I'll catch one or two fish a day and do nothing.' He laughs and lies back, pulling his giggling children on top of him. His wives stop plucking chicken feathers and glance over at him, smiling. Blabasy, I see, is quite the family man.

We eat a big, filling dinner of chicken and rice. To top it off, Blabasy's sister brings over a calabash of freshly squeezed cow's milk from the village. I notice that the family eats every part of the chicken, tendons, skin and all, spitting out the bones into a bowl. I try to follow their example, aware that I'm used to being finicky and wasteful when I eat chicken back home. Here, killing a chicken is only done on special occasions, for the arrival of an honoured guest. It is a luxury.

I'm grateful I never made it to Mopti, as being with this family is a delight. I could never have predicted such a treat when Blabasy called to me from his lone hut on the bank. It's quite a contrast to my unpleasant experience in Koa the other evening.

Blabasy turns on his tiny transistor radio and West African music floods the night. He pulls out his own foam mattress for me to sleep on, and none of my protestations will convince him to keep it for himself. I sit beside him and his kids, and we all look down the slope at the Niger flowing past in the silver moonlight. The waves make a slurping, *slap-slap* sound on the mud bank below, stars blazing above. His wives sit down by the hut, nursing their babies and staring at the opposite shore which makes only the faintest imprint in the darkness. The transistor radio drones on weakly, trying to be heard in all this immensity.

Sunrise is one of the best times to paddle in West Africa. It's before the midday heat, before most villagers wake up. Wildlife revels at this time of the morning. Four-foot-long monitor lizards crawl from the water and creep behind brush. Fish pluck at insects on the water's surface. And birds – thousands of them – fly in unbroken, undulating clouds that dip and shoot across the river. These flocks are expertly formed, not a single bird out of place, all flying with careful yet carefree precision. A cloud of them flies overhead now – that is the only word for it, a cloud – and they curl and bend in the shape of a gigantic snake, completely blocking out the sun and causing a shadow to fall over me. I stop paddling and raise my eyes to the extraordinary cacophony above. I watch the individual birds, gliding in sync with the rest of the group, no-one straggling, no-one breaking away. The cloud swoops towards a tree and lands all at once, the branches filled with fluttering bodies, becoming instantly alive with song. I feel the futility of trying to take in the beauty of such a scene, and so I just gape for a while, a child again.

I paddle on through the morning, not seeing a single

person in a canoe to break the long spread of river before me. Perhaps this is because a storm is starting to rise, so I paddle hard, wanting to make as much distance as possible towards Mopti before it comes. Storms tend to appear from the north-west, spending hours taking over the sky with a looming darkness. I like to play guessing games with them, wondering if they'll hit me with rain or miss me altogether. Sometimes the distant thunderheads shoot out sparks of lightning, as if making threats. Other times they lose their nerve and drift over silently, sullenly, a light patter of rain hitting me in short-lived protest before moving on.

This time, though, I can tell it's going to be different. A great wind is already acting as harbinger for a big act to come, blowing directly against me, slowing my paddling to a crawl. Dark clouds boom and rattle, while great Saharan winds churn up the red clay soil and paint blood trails across the sky. I'm stuck in the middle of the river and rush towards shore. The winds are getting even worse, the river sloshing with three-foot-high whitecaps. It is the Jekyll–Hyde phenomenon of the Niger, the river utterly calm one moment, only to burst into waves and rapids the next. And here I am caught in the capriciousness yet again, struggling with my bad arm to nose the kayak into the waves and get across before the worst of the storm hits.

I lean forward to secure my bags, and a wave broadsides my boat and flips it over. I fall out and swim to the surface, seeing my kayak bottom up and speeding steadily away. I dive for it and grab its tail, turning it over and retrieving my paddle, only to see my little backpack – the one with passport, money, journal – starting to sink near by.

It is as if the worst of my fears are being realized, one after the other, but by treading water and holding on to the kayak, I'm able to retrieve the backpack. Pulling myself inside the boat, I fumble to get oriented in the midst of the waves and paddle towards shore with all my strength. Thunder bellows, lightning flashes. I make it to the bank, rain shooting from the sky with such force that the drops sting my skin. I huddle, shaking from adrenalin, and take a tally of what I lost: both water bottles and some packets of dried fruit, but, mercifully, nothing else. The Niger has won my submission.

I see a radio tower in the distance. Thank God: Mopti. My halfway point. It will be a dubious victory, though, with everything I own completely soaked from my kayak wipe-out, and myself not quite recovered from it. Physically, I'm wasted. Mentally, I have a new and formidable respect for the wrath of the Niger. I've never wanted to get somewhere so badly – except, maybe, to Timbuktu. I've been battling impatience again, my stomach rumbling from hunger, my arms aching after a long day of paddling. In these circumstances, Mopti feels like a bastion of air-conditioning, agreeable meals and, most of all, rooms with doors that lock: things I've grudgingly done without.

My journey on the river is inevitably teaching me humility. I am learning that the body can survive on basic foods, and that they needn't taste or look good to perform their task of quieting the stomach and providing nourishment. Even the smallest things that I take for granted in the West are nearly impossible-to-find luxuries along the Niger – lavatories, telephones, a private place to bathe. After a while of this 'doing without', I start to trade the world back home for this one. I start to see, with glaring clarity, how little I actually do need, and how strongly the West tries to convince me otherwise. All those commercials back home, all those advertisements for designer clothes, scented toilet paper, Home Shopping Club miscellany. We're taught to think we need certain things if we are to be comfortable, safe, happy. And so it's all about fear. Fear of having the 'wrong' rather than the 'right' things, fear of not having as much as the next guy, fear of what we look like or how we sound. The endless fears. And yet, if I'm honest with myself, I see that I've been carrying in my little kayak all that I truly need: food, water, a couple of changes of clothes, medicine, a tent for shelter. The few luxuries I do have are superfluous, and they will remain buried deep in my backpack to be unearthed when I eventually head back home. The digital tape recorder. The CD player. The Faulkner novel. No use for any of those things here.

Mopti looks sizeable as I approach it, large villages lining the banks of the Niger on both sides, people screaming at me to paddle over to them and give them *cadeaux*. I cut across the Niger towards the central part of town. Most boats head to the main dock, where scores of people gather to sell their wares along the river's shore. There are the enormous slabs of greyish Saharan salt. Mangoes, bananas, fried rice cakes, kola nuts. Pots and pans, flip-flops, writing supplies. Each merchant has his speciality. Every conceivable thing is represented.

I decide to avoid the crowds of the docks by stopping to the north of town. I land my kayak near a group of women washing clothes in the river, their feet submerged in a thick brown mud that smells strongly of human refuse and animal dung. Littering the shore is the typical detritus of cities – snack wrappers, broken bottles, discarded shoes. I pull my kayak out of the muck and stand on solid ground, taking a deep breath. Mopti. Finally. It seems miraculous to be here. Distant Timbuktu feels not so distant any more.

I deflate my kayak for the first time since leaving Old Ségou. It shrinks into a simple piece of rubber. This rubber has, amazingly, kept me afloat through storms and heat and crowds, getting me and my things as far as Mopti. I can barely believe it.

Kids surround me, standing so close that I constantly have to say *pardon* in order to move. I fold up the kayak and put it in its bag, smelly mud covering my arms and dirtying my backpack and paddle. I try to rinse off in the Niger, but my feet just sink into muck up to my shins. I'm supposed to get a room at the Kananga Hotel in order to meet Rémi, so I hoist my bags to my shoulders and carry them to a nearby road to get a taxi. I wait for a while, only to look up and see the hotel sitting across the street from me. Like serendipity.

It turns out that the Kananga is Mopti's only luxury hotel. As I enter the lobby, a French couple, sitting in rattan chairs and sipping cocktails, looks at me with surprise and derision. I squeeze my bags through the main door, leaving mud smears on the plate glass. I can't imagine what I look like. I've come to forget all notions of personal appearance by now, accepting the omnipresent mud on me, the dirty sandals, the wet skirt, the sweaty T-shirt. This is simply the way things are when you've been kayaking on the Niger for a while.

French families leaving the dining room frown at me, their blond-haired children gaping and pointing. If there's one thing I'm used to by now, it's being gaped at. Fortunately, the Malian concierge doesn't seem fazed by what I look like. She smiles at me in the same way she smiles at the other guests, and there's nothing disingenuous about her expression of good will; she knows – as I do – that this posh hotel is just one, albeit comfortable, version of the world. I do catch her look of surprise when I open my muddy backpack to pull out a huge wad of damp Malian cash, courtesy of the National Geographic Society. I feel like some kind of illegal arms dealer. The French couple nearby notices this, too: the incongruity of a grubby woman emerging from the river, mud-smeared and greasy-haired, having a huge roll of bills. I promptly get a room. And a hot shower. I plan to sleep as if I had no intention of waking.

# CHAPTER SEVEN

THE HOTEL STAFF RECOMMEND TO ME A LOCAL MAN named Assou, a well-respected friend of the Peace Corps folk in town who knows about conditions along the Niger from Mopti to Timbuktu. He enters the hotel lobby, sporting a loudly patterned red silk shirt and sunglasses. We shake hands and the sunglasses come off, and I see a man with sensitive, intelligent eyes and shyness in his expression. There is also a precocious air about him, exhibited in his uncanny ability to speak English. Though he's only twenty-eight, he speaks the best, most colloquial English I've yet heard in Mali, and he knows German, French, Spanish – even a little Japanese. He is also a prodigious talker, the simplest question from me eliciting a twenty-minute response.

We sit down for a while – for him to talk, me to listen. He tells me that his greatest claim to fame is having been a guide for Tom Robbins who vacationed in West Africa, and he begins to tell me much more about the author than I ever wanted to know, everything from how Robbins visited a particular Dogon tribe to his penchant for hard-boiled eggs.

'He is a very famous American writer,' Assou declares, at the end of what has become a half-hour tale. 'Am I right?'

'Sort of,' I say.

'He sent me a letter. It's true. I'll show it to you.' He wants to get a taxi so he can show me the letter right now, back in his office. It's that important to him, proving his affiliation and friendship with Robbins. I promise him I'll see the letter later. If I remember. When I mention my trip down the Niger and what it's been like so far, Assou says I obviously didn't know about the genies that inhabit the river – every Malian knows about them – which explains why I've been having problems. It's not uncommon, he says, for people to simply disappear when travelling on the river. Even the most experienced boatmen have been known to vanish, with no trace of their bodies, the genies taking them. Genies themselves live in the eddies and rapids. They control the wind and current, and they alone decide whether they'll let a person pass. He says it's essential that I enlist these spirits to my cause of reaching Timbuktu, or who knows what tragedies might befall me.

At his urging, I agree to meet with him this evening to see a sorcerer for a consultation about my trip. Such consultations with sorcerers and witches are routine for most West Africans, Muslim or not. Fetishism and superstition are as alive and well in the twenty-first century as they were during Park's time, nearly everyone wearing *saphies*, or magic charms, meant to ward off evil and ensure success in myriad endeavours. Park could not help remarking on the charms: 'These *saphies* are prayers or rather sentences, from the Koran, which the Mahomedan priests write on scraps of paper and sell to the simple natives, who consider them to possess extraordinary virtues. I did not meet with a man who was not fully persuaded of the powerful efficacy of these amulets.' The Koranic verses are sewn inside little leather pouches, made by special *saphie* makers, and there is such a demand for encasing the verses that these craftsmen have made a good living for centuries. Assou, an avowed agnostic, still trusts his luck to the *saphie* that he hides beneath his shirt. He shows it to me with a smile of embarrassment, shrugging. Better not to take any chances.

Fetishism is another part of West African culture that hasn't changed much since Park's time, and Assou admits that he fears those who practise it. Every large town has its own fetish market, and Mopti is no exception. People in Mali widely believe that sacrificing live animals, or otherwise making ritual use of some part of one, be it the fur, skin, teeth or bones, has magical utility. The fetish object is brought to a local witch doctor, who then performs a spell for the client. Invoking the powers of a dead chameleon might bring fortune for a child. Sacrificing a goat might bring success in business. But animals aren't the only victims; occasionally, people are murdered for the purposes of voodoo. Women have been found dead on the streets of Mopti with their breasts removed for special spells.

Would-be politicians, wanting a guarantee that they'll win an election, have arranged for the sacrifice of albino men or women. This latter fact sounded incredible to me until Assou introduced me to the music of Salif Keita, one of West Africa's most celebrated musicians, who also happened to be an albino. Keita, who was rejected by his superstitious father (albinos are often associated with malign spirits), found himself living on the streets of Bamako. He wrote songs about his predicament there, which included being hunted by men needing albinos to sacrifice. Apparently, it had got so bad during the national elections that he had no choice but to flee Mali.

I leave Assou to check out Mopti for a while. It's the most comfortable place I've experienced in this country, with plenty of amenities at convenient distances from each other. There are a couple of Arab-run clothing stores offering Internet access. A pastry shop sells frosted cake tasting remarkably close to the real thing. The large tourist market beats Bamako's and is filled with an impressive array of exorbitantly priced old African trade beads. There is also the kitsch of all touristy places in Africa: zebra-skin sandals and wallets, cowhide drums, cheap antelope carvings darkened with shoe polish. Every once in a while some more interesting items emerge: silver Tuareg Koran-holders, Dogon amulets, old brass sculptures. Tribal masks are omnipresent, with about eight prototypical designs found in most of the stalls. This selection satisfies the majority of tourists, though there will be the occasional connoisseur trying to find 'a real antique'. They do better looking in African art galleries back home; the best Malian merchants can do is sell them thirty-year-old ones, along with the dubious promise that they were 'actually used'.

I learn not to touch or gaze at anything for too long in these stalls, as hawkers will follow me halfway across Mopti as soon as I show even mild interest in something. They become incensed and impatient when I tell them that I have very little money to part with. I don't bother to explain that, by US government standards, I've lived below the poverty level for much of my adult life as a graduate student, surviving on a trifle from teaching and magazine writing (not to mention selling my platelets). These dealers have cars much nicer than my fourteen-year-old Toyota Corolla, own vast quantities of rare trade beads, live in large houses filled with Western goods. But the minute I say I'm American, it's as if a transformation has occurred before their eyes, and I become some kind of Rich Foreigner with endless supplies of cash. There is nothing I can say that will modify this image they have of me; it's utterly pointless to argue with them.

I decide to look up Peace Corps Baba to see one of the best African art collections in Mali. His real name is Oumar Cisse, but Moptians coined his new name due to his close relations with the Peace Corps folk in town. Baba is something of a Malian celebrity: the Lonely Planet *West Africa* guide gives him top billing, and he sold an antique Dogon door to none other than Henry Louis Gates Jr, the renowned Afro-American cultural historian, who came to

Mali on his *Wonders of the African World* tour a few years ago. All the taxi drivers know of 'Peace Corps Baba' by name, and apparently no trip to Mopti is complete without paying him a visit.

I find Baba in the middle of treating an older French couple and their teenage daughter to a lavish meal on the roof of his two-storey building. Baba invites me to join them. The French daughter, I notice, looks on the verge of vomiting. She holds her stomach and lets out feeble complaints about the spices in a dish, while Baba ignores her completely and brags to us about all the places he's seen in Europe. He's one of Mali's biggest exporters of African trade beads, and they've made him rich. He now spends most of his time travelling all over the world to gem and bead shows. He tells me that he goes to America only during the summer because he can't abide cold weather; he absolutely refuses to get anywhere near snow. He clutches himself and shakes his head.

'You could buy a coat,' I suggest. 'Maybe an Arctic parka.'

He starts talking about Big Macs and fat women, and I excuse myself to head back to town. I'll look at his art some other time.

I wander along Mopti's riverfront. I'm grateful that I'm not on the Niger today as I'd be battling my way through heavy wind and waves. Not to mention that Mopti provides a nice, comfortable break that I'd like to extend for a while. The city is prosperous, with forty thousand people, spread out over a mile along the Niger and expanding inland into the savannah. The French built Mopti to its present bustling state, and it's full of colonial-era whitewashed cement buildings, paved but potholed streets, and a healthy Peace Corps population teaching, among other things, hand-washing. Mopti has also become the headquarters for many of Mali's most successful travel agencies and touring companies – which might explain why I can't walk even a few feet without being assailed by a guide trying to book me for a tour. Apparently there are pottery villages, colour-ful tribes, breathtaking scenery, all awaiting me. And how about a boat tour on the Niger?

'I do *not*,' I tell the young man who suggested this last choice, 'need a boat tour on the Niger.'

But the fact that I have spoken at all is taken as encouragement, and he joins me at my restaurant table as I order fish and chips. My meal promptly arrives, and I dip a French fry in some ketchup, giving terse answers to his litany of questions – the same tedious questions that precede all Mopti tour pitches. What's my name? Where am I from? How long in Mali?

'Look,' I say, sighing, 'can we just get to the point?'

'I have an all-day boat tour for you,' he says in poor English. 'You take a boat, see the Niger. The Niger is very nice.'

'You may not believe this,' I say, 'but I've already seen the Niger.'

'You will go in my company's *pinasse*,' he says. 'It's very comfortable. It's a nice boat.'

'I already have my own boat.'

'No! How is this possible?'

I shrug. 'I brought it from home. It's in my hotel room.'

'In Africa, it's not good to tell lies,' he says.

'I'm not lying. It's a red inflatable boat, and it's in my hotel room.'

He stands up. He's actually getting angry with me. 'I want to help you. That's all. I want you to have a nice boat tour. And what do you do? You tell me lies. Do you know? The Niger is a very beautiful river.'

'I'm sure it is,' I tell him.

No trip to Mali is complete without seeing its most famous tourist attraction after Timbuktu: the Great Mosque in the city of Djenné. A UNESCO world heritage site, it also has the distinction of being the largest mud building in the world. Djenné is about ninety miles south-west of Mopti, on its own little island in the Bani River. I decide to get there by *taxi brousse*, the most popular and cheapest means of travel in Mali. These vehicles are nothing more than small, ancient Toyota trucks with wooden benches in the back covered by a metal frame and tarp. Hundreds of them converge on the outskirts of town, in a large dirt parking area. Always on the alert, would-be passengers surround the first empty trucks that pull in. When the drivers announce their destinations, the crowds overrun the vehicles and rush to get inside, creating a shoving, crashing stampede of bodies.

I arrive early in the morning in order to have a better

chance of claiming a choice corner-bench spot for myself. My strategy works. People soon start to fill in after me. The *taxi brousse* doesn't leave until it's 'full', though what constitutes 'full' is a matter of individual opinion. Drivers will squeeze in as many human bodies as can be fitted inside, barring suffocation. I try as best I can to stake out my bench territory, creating a vice with my thighs and mounting a full-body resistance to the seizure of my precious space, but this proves futile. Before long, my right thigh is sitting on someone else's, my feet are in some woman's lap, and a baby is perched on my shoulders. For a truck bed that couldn't be larger than six feet by five feet, I count an extraordinary thirty-two bodies inside, not including the two guys hanging out the back.

At last, after an hour of cramming and crowding, the truck is ready to leave. That it can move at all is a miracle, but it finally groans out of the parking lot, shudders, and gains momentum on the road, flying along at breakneck speed. I try not to imagine an all-too-common scenario in this country: our sardine-packed *taxi brousse* taking a bend too quickly, overturning, and reducing the truck and its occupants to a pile of twisted metal and hamburger meat.

Across the aisle are two Belgian backpackers; the woman sits awkwardly on her boyfriend's lap, her feet dangling in the face of a small boy crouched on the floor.

'What brings you to Mali?' she asks me from behind several heads.

'I'm going to be writing an article.'

'So this is your *job*?' the boyfriend says incredulously.

I extract a hand to wipe the sweat from my eyes. 'Yeah,' I say.

'I don't think I want your job,' the woman says, frowning.

It takes us an incredible six hours to travel the ninety miles to Djenné, our truck finally stopping beside the Bani River with Djenné resting on an island before us. Accounting for our long delay were numerous stops to load and offload passengers, which meant the tedious packing and repacking of bodies inside. We're all ordered out so the driver can make it across a muddy tract to the ferry. We try not to step on any limbs as we carefully extract ourselves. I long ago lost all feeling in my legs, and I immediately start up a dance to restore circulation. I'm particularly grateful that the baby on my shoulders has been removed. Just after we left Mopti it'd dirtied its nappy, and its mother had been unable to attend to it until now. The result had been a miserable child and a smelly diaper congealing for hours in the Saharan heat. Everyone inside the truck had had to endure the inescapable, pungent shit smell. After all this, Djenné had better be good. All I know is that I'll pay whatever it costs to charter a car back to Mopti.

We wait another hour for the ferry, the clouds unleashing a downpour that turns everything underfoot to deep mud. At last the ferry arrives and we get on, crossing the Bani. We crowd back into the truck for the final ride into town – but not before the Belgians and I, being *tubabs*, are charged an exorbitant fee to enter the city. The fee reminds

*Above*: In front of the usual crowd of onlookers, I load my gear into the kayak and prepare to leave Koa.

*Below*: My kayak being held for safe-keeping in the Fulani village of Guro.

I always greatly feared being caught in one of the Niger's great storms.